The Believers' Eternal Rest

There remains, then, a Sabbath-rest for the people of God.
(Hebrews 4:9)

***

Myrrh
Books
Overland Park, Kansas

The Believers' Eternal Rest
An Interpretation of Richard Baxter's The Saints' Everlasting Rest

John D. Gillespie

ISBN: 9781794184893

Library of Congress Control Number: 2019900609

Special thanks to Nell Riechers and Ellie Lee for editing this manuscript.

Contents

Foreword by Ian Coffey

A Book With a Strange Beginning

Chapter One *What Is Our Eternal Rest?* 1

Chapter Two *Our Rest Defined* 6

Chapter Three *Before We Proceed* 12

Chapter Four *Understanding This Rest* 25

Chapter Five *Four Foundations of Our Rest* 43

Chapter Six *Reason Tells Us of the Wonders of Our Rest* 55

Chapter Seven *The Wonders of Our Rest* 65

Chapter Eight *Who Receives God's Rest?* 92

Chapter Nine *Six Truths About Heaven Proven by the Bible* 98

Chapter Ten *Why Can't We Have Heaven Now?* 105

Chapter Eleven *Will Our Spirits Enjoy This Rest Before Our Bodies are Resurrected?* 111

Chapter Twelve *Our Privilege to Help Others Toward Heaven* 115

Chapter Thirteen *Motivation for a Heaven-Minded Life* 129

Chapter Fourteen   *Hindrances to a Heavenly Life* 153

Chapter Fifteen   *Helping You Live a Heavenward Life* 165

Chapter Sixteen   *Meditating on Heaven* 177

Chapter Seventeen   *Helps for Meditating on Heaven* 189

Chapter Eighteen   *Preaching to Yourself* 199

Chapter Nineteen   *Be Encouraged!* 209

Appendix   Richard Baxter's Introductory Letter to His Parish 213

Afterword by David Bhadreshwar

Foreword

Are you curious?

When someone tells you a surprise awaits, do you find yourself imagining what it might be? Do you lie awake excited at the prospect of what tomorrow might bring? Are you eager to know what lies in store, beyond the horizon?

Jesus spoke to his disciples shortly before he was betrayed and crucified. Anticipating the heartbreak and fear this would provoke, he made a solemn promise of hope:

Let not you hearts be troubled. Believe in God, believe also I me. In my Father's house are many rooms. If it were not so, would I have told you I go to prepare a place for you? And if I go and prepare a place for you, I will come again and will take you to myself, that where I am you may be also. And you know the way to the place where I am going.
(John 14:1-4)

I ask the question again: are you curious? Would you like to know something of what Jesus meant by this astonishing promise? What does the "Father's house" look like? Where is it located? What did Jesus mean by, "I go and prepare a place for you"?

The book you are reading sets out to answer these questions from the pages of Scripture and explains something of what Bishop N.T. Wright has described as "life, after life after death".

In short, it's a book for those curious to know what happens next.

John Gillespie joins tens of thousands who have personally profited from a book written almost 400 years ago by a thirty year old Christian Pastor, told he only had a short time to live. With eternity beckoning, he felt the need to study what the Bible has to say about life after death and he set about his work with a passion. Read on if you want to learn what transpired.

This book, it its original form, is the fruit of this young Pastor's personal journey of discovering what the Bible has to say about the life to come. It's not based on speculation about the paranormal, nor personal 'out of body' experiences but a detailed exploration of what the Word of God reveals about Heaven. It is essentially a book for the curious Christian keen to discover something of what God has in store in the life to come.

Reading this manuscript I have been personally challenged by several thoughts. First, I recognise I am too earth-anchored in my understanding. You have heard the phrase, "So heavenly minded but no earthly use". I wonder if the reverse is more accurate, "So earthly minded but no heavenly use"? Paul the apostle, urged a congregation of young believers to, "..seek the things that are above, where Christ is, seated at the right hand of God" (Colossians 3:1). That can be translated "mind heavenly things" and points us to the need of a bigger, broader perception of why we are here on earth. If my vision extends no further than my next vacation or retirement plans then the question, "What next?" is simply pushed to the edge of my understanding. This evidences an earth-anchored mentality which produces a stunted spirituality.

Secondly, I am struck by how much the Bible has to say about the afterlife and yet how rarely it is preached about from our pulpits. I struggle to recall the last time I heard a sermon about Heaven and I confess (with shame) that it has not featured as much as it should in my own preaching. Is this surely, further proof of an earth-anchored outlook?

Thirdly, something that comes out in this paraphrased treatment of Baxter's masterpiece, is how this teaching about the life to come is so practical and applied. If you think this book is 'other worldly' – think again! These pages are a manual on discipleship that teach us how to live now in the light of the world to come. You will discover fresh insights into what it means to follow Jesus with a single-minded passion and to serve him in today's world.

My friend, John Gillespie is to be commended for the work he has put into bringing this valuable book to a new generation of followers of Christ. Read it and be challenged, changed and blessed.

And get hungry for Heaven!

Rev Ian Coffey MTh
Vice Principal, Moorlands College,
Dorset, England.
January 2019.

A Book With a Strange Beginning

Have you ever known someone to write a book to himself?

A reminder note, yes...
    Perhaps a letter....
        But an entire book?

Sometime around 1645 a thirty-year-old pastor was told he had very little time left to live. Wisely, he determined he had better do some serious thinking about death and Heaven since he was so soon to encounter both. Being far from home and alone, with nothing but a Bible, paper and a quill, he began to write. He wrote for the next six months. The result was *800,000* words about eternity (just for perspective, you are holding about 65,000 words in your hand). He in fact did not die soon. He went on the live another forty-five years, writing some 140 more books. [1]

But the book he wrote to himself became Richard Baxter's most enduring and helpful. Given to the public in 1650, for many years *The Saints' Everlasting Rest* was to sell 3,000 copies annually and go through twelve editions in Richard's lifetime.

We have his own words on the origins of his greatest work:

Being in my quarters far from home, cast into extreme languishing by the sudden loss of about a gallon of blood, and after many years of foregoing weakness, and having no acquaintance about me, nor any books but my Bible, and living in constant expectation of death, I bent my thoughts on my Everlasting Rest; and because my

---

[1] So prolific was he that he earned the nickname "Scribbling Dick." J.I Packer, *The Saints' Everlasting Rest,* (Vancouver: Regent College Publishing, 2004), vii.

memory, through extreme weakness, was imperfect, I took my pen and began to draw up my own funeral sermon, or some helps for my own meditation of Heaven, to sweeten both the rest of my life and my death. ... I began to write ... intending but the quantity of a sermon or two ... but being in continued weakness, where I had no books nor better employment, I followed on till it was enlarged to the bulk in which it was published.[2]

What a blessing it has been to the wider Christian world that Richard Baxter was told he was soon to die! God gave him grace to focus on what mattered most. Having one foot in the grave did him, and consequently many others, everlasting good.

Not many good books on Heaven have been written of late. We are, on the one hand, an earth-bound culture which has a hard time thinking past the weekend, let alone into Eternity. Randy Alcorn's *Heaven* is superb.[3] Bruce Milne has written a very good commentary in *The Bible Speaks Today* series.[4] I am sure some other good books are out there, but they are few and far between. On the other hand, we are a strangely gullible generation which - while ignoring God - is yet desperate for some sort of proof of something beyond ourselves. Hence, more than a few books are flying off the shelves these days - anecdotal rather than biblical stories of near death visits to "heaven." While they do fascinate, I am not sure that all of them are helpful.

Baxter's book really belongs on a shelf all its own. There is not another like it. Do not look for a comprehensive systematic

---

[2] Cited in the *Introductory Essay* by John Thomas Wilkinson,. *The Saints' Everlasting Rest,* by Richard Baxter. Edited and Introduced by John T Wilkinson with Foreword by J.I. Packer. Abridgement copyright 1962 Methodist Publishing House. 2004 edition by Regent College Publishing, Vancouver, p.2.

[3] Randy Alcorn, *Heaven* (Carol Stream: Tyndale Momentum, 2004).

[4] Bruce Milne, *The Message of Heaven and Hell* (Downers Grove: IVP, 2002).

theology of Heaven within its pages. It is not there. Baxter does not divide things into neat categories: death, the intermediate state, the resurrection of our bodies, the renewal of all things. That is not his purpose. Alcorn and Milne will do that for you. What Baxter does is go for your heart, via your mind. He is concerned that we raise our thoughts and then our affections heavenward. He wants us to be ready to die and spend eternity with Jesus. He sees in the Bible enough information about Heaven to fill our thoughts and ignite our hearts.

Baxter is not aiming simply to impart facts. He wants us to *long* for the presence of God. He is convinced, both from the Bible and from his own experience, that we can begin to "visit Heaven" now. Not in some spooky sense. Not via a séance or trance. But quite simply and wonderfully by taking onboard biblical information about Heaven and – with the help of the Holy Spirit – thinking about it until it affects our hearts. Meditating on Jesus and His Heaven is, for Baxter, not an option for a Christian, but an art, and an essential, happy duty.

For Scribbling Dick, Heaven-mindedness honours God, leads to courageous living for Jesus today, and broadsides sin. His book is not mere speculation, but the testimony of a dying man who learned how to prepare for Heaven every day. It is rich in theology and practice. It is experiential Christianity at its best.

Understanding Richard Baxter

Three things shaped Richard Baxter and the writing of *The Saints' Everlasting Rest.*

First, and as he stated above, was his – not unfounded – belief that he was soon to die. God graced him with a startling vision of his own demise. Days and weeks and months in physical agony were turned to good for him and for thousands after him. He learned how to think about Heaven in such vividness that he could refer to it as walking in the New Jerusalem and living in the suburbs of Heaven. This was not for him some strange mysticism, but simple meditation upon the truths of the Bible regarding our Rest in Jesus.

Next, the English Civil War (1642-51) was being waged all about him. Death and agony were inescapable. Forgive his spelling and hear him:

O the sad and heart-piercing spectacles that mine eyes have seen in four years [sic] space! In this fight, a dear friend fall[s] down by me; [in] another, a precious Christian brought home wounded or dead; scarce a moneth, scare a week without the sight or noise of bloud. Surely there is none of this in Heaven. Our eyes shall then be filled no more with, nor our hearts be filled with such sights as *Worcester, Edg-hil, Newbury, Nantwich, Montgomery* ... My eyes shall never more behold the earth covered with the carcasses of the slain ...[5]

The tragedy of war and the constancy of death had pushed Baxter's heart heavenward. His rich pastoral ministry in Kidderminster having been interrupted by the War, Baxter gave himself to ministering to soldiers as a chaplain. He lived through horrific scenes, processing them through his living faith in Jesus and his vibrant hope of Heaven. In this role he labored for more than two years until broken in body. Yet his confidence in God, the Gospel, and Heaven held him in the face of such a display of human depravity. It was faith, not cynicism, which grew within.

Third, Richard Baxter was troubled by the "antinomianism"[6] of his day. A cheapening of grace was producing a laziness and

---

[5] Wilkinson, p.6.

worldly spirit among God's people. Bear this in mind when you read anything Baxter writes, for he writes with vehemence and with an emphasis on human responsibility not often seen today. He was a wise pastor, and seeing the disease of irresponsible worldliness among the churches, he prescribed the medicines of diligence and deliberate attention to one's spiritual well-being.

The Calvinists of his day thought him too concerned with human responsibility. But for Baxter, grace did not rock one to sleep until waking in Heaven, but prepared one for battle until victory in Heaven. Hence you have in *The Saints' Everlasting Rest* a book which presents not only the full and sure promises of God, but the essential duties of the Heaven-bound Christian.

In such a world Richard Baxter lived - with Heaven and Hell in full view. It was he who spoke the potent words, the sentiment of which almost all evangelical preachers used to repeat:

I preached as never sure to preach again, and as a dying man to dying men.

How we need to learn from such men! There was such a sobriety, such a joy, such an urgency, such a peace. Richard Baxter emerged from his grave illness a better follower of Jesus and a better pastor and preacher. He was able to see the entire trial as God's providential occurrence for his good, and for the good of his congregation, for that laborious illness gave birth to a timeless book:

---

[6] Literally "against law." Antinomianism asserts that in being saved by grace, one need not give serious regard to morality or Christian conduct.

I offer up my thanks to the merciful God who ... interrupted my public labours for a time, that he might force me to do you a more permanent service, which, else, I had never like to have attempted ...[7]

Having produced his 800,000 words in a literary blink of an eye (six months), he was aware of the unpolished nature of his book. In his introductory letter to his beloved flock in Kidderminster, he warned them of the book's imperfections:

Much less may you wonder if the whole be very imperfect, seeing it was written, as it were with one foot in the grave, by a man that was betwixt the living and the dead.[8]

I have reproduced Baxter's warm and wonderful introductory letter in the Appendix and I would urge you to read it before you read my offering.

My Source

Eight hundred thousand words! Thankfully, others have given us abridgments of Baxter's original, most notably John Wesley in 1754. John T. Wilkinson gave us his remarkable abridgement in 1962. Wilkinson brought 800,000 words down to 80,000. The words are all Baxter's but Wilkinson had to do some serious surgery. While entire sections were removed, Wilkinson managed to give us Baxter's heart for and theology of Heaven without compromise.

I first read Wilkinson's abridgment of Baxter's book in 2007 while preparing a sermon series on Heaven. Now dog-eared and well-worn, Wilkinson's labour of love has been my main source in producing this new interpretation.

---

[7] Richard Baxter, p. 24
[8] p. 23.

My Purpose and Method in Rewriting Baxter's Book

I have rewritten Baxter's book because I want you to discover Jesus and the Heaven He is preparing for you. Few today will read the original, perhaps a few may read my re-launch. We ignore Heaven to our poverty. So, having been blessed by the original, I offer you Baxter's book in the form of a new interpretation.

Here is how I have attempted the project: First, I have endeavored to remain faithful to Baxter's theology and heart. That has been of utmost importance to me. I have to meet him one day! It has been my hope that something of his fire has come through the centuries, from his pen and heart to my word processor and heart, and to you.

Second, I have not worked word by word, or sentence by sentence, or even page by page, but idea by idea. My method has been to seek to understand Baxter's heart and thought and represent - and re-present - them to you. Being an interpretation, this book is totally mine, while seeking to be faithful to the man who inspired it. So, while it is my work, and I bear the responsibility for it, I am hopeful that you can read it and get what Richard Baxter would have wanted you to get had you read his.

Richard Baxter, like his Puritan brothers, was nothing if not thorough. Their writings can easily come across as tedious to us moderns with our shrunken brains and byte-size attention spans. Even Wilkinson's abridgment can seem at times repetitive. I have tried to trim this up a little, but not too much, as I have wanted to remain faithful to Richard, and humble enough to consider that if he thought something worth repeating, who am I to think otherwise? So, if you find yourself thinking "he already said that!" take it as something you probably need to hear again!

I have added many more Bible passages than Richard, and many, if not most, of the illustrations are mine and not his. My interpretation took on a life of its own, and I found along the way that I too, like Richard, was writing a book to myself, for I have also have been graced to face my own mortality, and it is past time for me to get serious about Heaven.

It is a strange attribute of our schizophrenic age that – all the while claiming to be too secular and sophisticated for anything beyond our tiny selves - we will nevertheless watch endless movies and television shows about "death and the hereafter," read countless books and articles searching for clues into "the afterlife," be forever fascinated by the paranormal, nod our heads in approval at most any talking head who comes along and spouts his opinion about "the other side," and yet think someone strange who actually believes what *Jesus* says about Himself, ourselves, Heaven and Hell. Our secular age does not believe in nothing, it believes in anything and everything ... just as long as repentance and moral reformation are not required: "Bring on Valhalla, dish out the Nirvana, but don't give us any of this Jesus foolishness!" Well, as unfashionable as it may be, Richard Baxter will help you see that becoming well acquainted with Jesus and His Heaven is the most important thing that you can do.

Get ready to have your thinking rearranged and your upside down world turned right side up. This book will do that for you. Living in the constant sunlight of Jesus and Heaven will remind the Christ-follower that this life – no matter how pleasant or hard it may be – *is as bad as it will get for you.* Jesus and His Heaven awaits. For the Christ-refuser, this life – no

xi

matter how pleasant or hard – *is as good as it gets for you.* Jesus and His Judgment awaits.

I certainly commend his book to you as well as mine, and if you like his more, that is fine with me! What matters is that we begin to live today like Heaven bound followers of Jesus, being transformed by a rich view of what Jesus has purchased and is preparing for us.

Yet I am always with you;
you hold me by my right hand.
You guide me with your counsel,
and afterwards you will take me into glory.

Whom have I in heaven but you?
And earth has nothing I desire besides you.
My flesh and my heart may fail,
but God is the strength of my heart
and my portion forever.
(Psalm 73:23-26)

John Gillespie
January 2019
Overland Park, Kansas

Aim at Heaven and you will get Earth 'thrown in':
aim at Earth and you will get neither.

C.S. Lewis

*H*ow little comfort do all things in this world afford to a departing soul! My constant prayer for you to God shall be that all things may be below Him in your hearts, and that you may thoroughly master and mortify the desires of the flesh, and may live above in the Spirit, with the Father of spirits, till you arrive among the perfected spirits of the just.

Your much obliged servant,

Rich. Baxter

To Jesus

Chapter One

What Is Our Eternal Rest?

When Adam rebelled (and we happily joined in), we lost more than we realize. More than just our desire to know God, we lost our very ability to know Him. We naturally, without the awakening grace of God, neither *want to* nor *can* truly know God.

We today are so overfed on what does not nourish, so stuffed with meaningless tidbits, so fascinated by the trivial and time-bound that we have lost our appetite and aptitude for the nourishing, the meaningful, and the eternal.

We do not know what we are missing! Just like a poor man who has ceased to even dream of wealth or believe there can be anything better than his sad lot, so we, without Jesus opening the eyes of our hearts, are incapable of even imagining the joy and fullness which Jesus Christ has secured for us. When Jesus comes to us in the Gospel and makes known to us the wonders of salvation and the joys of eternity, He finds us spiritually dead in sin and blind to truth.

But He does not leave us that way!

It takes the supernatural, awakening grace of God to bring new life to dead sinners. And God sovereignly and wonderfully gives that grace.

The writer of the book in the Bible we call *Hebrews* reaches the mountaintop of his letter with these words: "There remains, then, a Sabbath-rest for the people of God." His letter – like the rest of the Bible - is written to dispel our ignorance of the wonderful salvation that we have in Jesus. In *Hebrews*, the entirety of our salvation might be summed up in this one word, *Rest.* Can you imagine a more wonderful hope to the weary man than Rest? All the labours and losses, the sadnesses and sorrows which we experience in this fallen life bring us to a longing for this Rest. There is no more welcome news than the promise of Rest for those wearied by the battle of life in this world. By "Rest" the Bible does not mean a lazy yawning through eternity. It is a wonderful word that speaks of a Heaven where we have finished forever with the constant and unavoidable battles – within us and all around us – of this fallen life. It speaks of a day coming when we will be released to become all that Jesus has created and redeemed us to be.

Dear reader, if you will give your best attention and your earnest desire to learn about God's Rest, then I promise you that you will not be disappointed by your journey of discovery, even as I have not been by mine. It is my prayer for you that this discovery will cause you to praise and worship God that He has not only been so merciful as to have a Rest for you, but so wonderful as to teach you now about what you can anticipate and expect.

God, through the Gospel and by His grace alone, undoes what Adam did, and opens our eyes to see, our minds to understand, and our hearts to desire what He has for us.

A Present and Future Rest

Now clearly the Rest spoken of at first means the rest from sin, and from religious self-effort to deal with our sin. Rest initially means the Rest of forgiveness and justification. When we, by the grace of God, believe in Jesus as Saviour we enter God's Rest. We cease from our religious efforts and our sinful rebellions, and come to Rest in the Gospel. But this Rest, though wonderful, is but the down-payment of the fullness of Rest which awaits. It is a foretaste of a feast to come!

This book is about the wonders of that Eternal Rest: Heaven itself.

Now in our desire to be a part of this Rest, we dare not fool ourselves with shallow hopes. You may be a member of a church. You might have grown up in a country or community where Christianity is all around you. Maybe you take communion, and consider yourself to be above the "enemies" of the Gospel. But, be careful! This Rest is not for the proud churchman, but for the humble believer! This Rest is for those who cast themselves wholly upon Jesus, trusting in His shed blood and nothing else to pay for their sins, abiding in Jesus as a branch does a vine, drawing all life from Him.

Not all who "go to church" are The Church. And not everyone who casually desires this Rest receives this Rest. (Who doesn't want to "go to Heaven"?) It is by turning from worthless things toward Jesus, and by our union with Him by faith that our place in Christ is secured and this Rest is received.

Jesus Himself offers this Rest!

All those the Father gives me will come to me, and whoever comes to me I will never drive away. For I have come down from heaven not to do my will but to do the will of him who sent me. And this is the will of him who sent me, that I shall lose none of all those he has given me, but raise them up at the last day. For my Father's will is that everyone who looks to the Son and believes in him shall have eternal life, and I will raise them up at the last day. (John 6:37-40)

3

But can we be *certain* that this Rest is for us? In other words, is it just a vague hope or a sure hope? Here is the Good News: The Believer in Jesus, weak as his faith may be, flawed as his walk may be, can surely trust in the unchangeable promise of God. You know that you are weak and failing. But do you know that He is strong and faithful? Our certain hope in the Rest that we have now through the forgiveness of sins, and will soon have in fullness in Heaven, is established on the promise and character of God Himself.

Scriptures to Ponder:

...being confident of this, that he who began a good work in you will carry it on to completion until the day of Christ Jesus. (Philippians 1:6)

To him who is able to keep you from stumbling and to present you before his glorious presence without fault and with great joy – to the only God our Saviour be glory, majesty, power and authority, through Jesus Christ our Lord, before all ages, now and for evermore! Amen. (Jude 24,25)

For those God foreknew he also predestined to be conformed to the image of his Son, that he might be the firstborn among many brothers and sisters. And those he predestined, he also called; those he called, he also justified; those he justified, he also glorified. (Romans 8:29,30)

Questions to Consider:

    1) Why is it necessary for God to awaken us by His grace if we are to even hunger for Him?

    2) When was the last time you thought about God's Eternal Rest, prepared for you?

3) What keeps you from hungering for Heaven?

4) How might this Rest be different from laziness?

Chapter Two

Our Rest Defined

As mentioned above, Rest refers first to the wonders of the Gospel which we receive the moment we believe in Jesus. To a soul troubled with guilt, chased by the Law, headed for a deserved judgment, the Gospel gives immediate rest and peace through the forgiveness of sin and the gift of Christ's righteousness.

That is the initial wonderful application of this word Rest.

But we are here looking beyond the immediate to the ultimate meaning of Rest. This is not in any way to diminish the wonder of the forgiveness of sins! Were it not for the wonders of God justifying sinners through the shed blood of Jesus on the Cross, we could have no hope of Heaven. Our salvation begins the very moment we believe the Gospel, but then grows brighter and brighter until it is complete in Heaven with all things being made new.

The path of the righteous is like the morning sun, shining ever brighter till the full light of day.
(Proverbs 4:18)

Rest means completion of the labour, the finishing of the course. It embraces the happiness of God into eternity, not just for the soul at the moment of death, but for the resurrected body at the end of history and for the renewal of all things.

This place or position of Rest, this eternal state for the Christian in Glory, will not be some passive - dare I say, boring

- existence. It will be a perfection or completion of that which began when we first believed. All sin will be gone, and we will be perfect in holiness (finally!). Our capacity to grow in knowledge and understanding will no longer be limited, but full. No longer hindered by sin, in Heaven we will be on an eternal journey of discovery, plumbing the depths of the riches of God forever. Our ability to worship God and to grow in our relationship with Him will be endlessly perfect. What has begun now in seed will then be in full flower. This can mean nothing less than our happiness being finally and forever complete.

For now we see only a reflection as in a mirror; then we shall see face to face. Now I know in part; then I shall know fully, even as I am fully known. (1 Corinthians 13:12)

Perfect happiness together in the presence of God! Happiness is what this present world strives and wars for but never grasps. This side of Heaven we may get a foretaste of perfect happiness, but only in Heaven will we enjoy the full feast of happiness. It is a foolish and vain hope to imagine that this present world, even at its best, can deliver what our hearts long for - complete and perfect happiness. Every good thing this world gives, if counted upon for that Rest which only God, the Gospel, and Heaven can give, will in the end leave us empty and frustrated.

We were made for more. We were made for God.

But a word of warning here. I have said it once, but I need to say it again: This happiness, this Rest, is for the Christian. Not just the churchman, or the person who holds a few Christian opinions. We are speaking here about the one who has harboured himself in Jesus and His Gospel and is willing to follow after Him.

Examine your heart and do not let yourself be content to talk like a Christian if you are not willing to walk like one. Don't expect to die the death of a believer if you are not willing to live the life of a believer! Sadly, the Bible warns us that many are resting on false hopes, believing that mere lip service to Jesus buys Heaven.

Not everyone who says to me, "Lord, Lord," will enter the kingdom of heaven, but only the one who does the will of my Father who is in heaven. (Matthew 7:21)

These people honour me with their lips, but their hearts are far from me. (Matthew 15:8)

Often, when a person dies, we speak of him as "being at peace," or we view his or her life as complete. But we are speaking of so much more here. We have been designed to inhabit eternity and the end which we have in view is not just the cessation of "animal life," but everlasting completion of the very purpose for which we have been created.

But I can almost hear some of you objecting: "Surely our ultimate purpose must be the Glory of God and not *our* Rest or happiness! This is just a selfish motive when God would have us live for a higher one!" I can understand this concern, and it deserves attention and a good answer.

It would be selfish if we viewed our Rest as something divorced from the Glory of God. It would be mercenary if we viewed our eternal happiness as wages for our labours. But when we see all this as the fruit of God's plan - to bring Glory to Himself in the gracious salvation of undeserving sinners,

8

making them eternally happy in Jesus, well, if the desire for such God-glorifying happiness is selfish, then let me be selfish!

I can also hear one or two saying that this pursuit of Heaven, of Rest, is nothing more than another form of legalism: "If you do this and that, then you will gain this happiness." Listen! Legalism does indeed say "Do this to gain that," but so does the Gospel. When the Gospel says, "Do this," it means: Believe in Jesus, seek Him, trust yourself wholly to His care, cease your own self-righteous efforts, follow Him as your Lord and King, deny yourself, be willing to suffer whatever comes your way. If we try through the keeping of rules to gain life, we are legalists. But if we trust in Jesus alone and respond to Him with our hearts and minds and bodies, we are not legalists.

The Gospel says "no" to earning but "yes" to effort!

Then they asked him, 'What must we do to do the works God requires?'
Jesus answered, 'The work of God is this: to believe in the one he has sent.'(John 6:28,29)

Then Jesus said to his disciples, 'Whoever wants to be my disciple must deny themselves and take up their cross and follow me.' (Matthew 16:24)

I certainly cannot argue with any who say that the glory of God must be the ultimate purpose we pursue. But what I want you to consider is that the salvation of sinners and the glory of God are not two things but one. And if God has made them one, we must not make them two! God is glorified in the salvation of sinners. Jesus – the Son of God - cares for the welfare of the sinner! He is the friend of sinners who came to seek the lost and to give His life as a ransom for many. Yet He also came to

9

do His Father's will and bring glory to His Father. Clearly, He saw the rescue of sinners and the bringing glory to His Father not in opposition to each other, but in concert. To us He is Saviour, Mediator, Redeemer, Reconciler, Intercessor, and to the Father He is the beloved Son, with whom the Father is well pleased.

Why are we so concerned with rest and happiness here, in this present life? Because we do not realize that true Rest and happiness cannot be known until we reach the goal and perfection of our salvation: Heaven itself. This is the end and aim of our journey, even as the Apostle Paul tells us:

For I am already being poured out like a drink offering, and the time for my departure is near. I have fought the good fight, I have finished the race, I have kept the faith. Now there is in store for me the crown of righteousness, which the Lord, the righteous Judge, will award to me on that day – and not only to me, but also to all who have longed for his appearing. (2 Timothy 4:6-8)

Just a thought for you to consider: Placing your Rest above, in Heaven with Jesus, not below with the passing things of this world, actually *frees you up* to properly love and enjoy this present world. So beware of the deadly idolatry of expecting from earth and others what only Heaven and Jesus can give: Rest. When you are no longer expecting from earth what only Heaven can give, and from people what only Jesus can give, you are free from bondage to idolatry, and thereby free to actually love and enjoy all that good things God has given you here and now. Your heart is above, safe and sound, and life here is put in perspective.

Thus, the Heaven-minded Christian is actually the freest person on earth.

Scriptures to Ponder:

But you have come to Mount Zion, to the city of the living God, the heavenly Jerusalem. You have come to thousands upon thousands of angels in joyful assembly, to the church of the firstborn, whose names are written in heaven. You have come to God, the Judge of all, to the spirits of the righteous made perfect, to Jesus the mediator of a new covenant, and to the sprinkled blood that speaks a better word than the blood of Abel. (Hebrews 12:22-24)

'Worthy is the Lamb, who was slain,
to receive power and wealth and wisdom and strength
and honour and glory and praise!'
Then I heard every creature in heaven and on earth and under
the earth and on the sea, and all that is in them, saying:
'To him who sits on the throne and to the Lamb
be praise and honour and glory and power,
for ever and ever!'
The four living creatures said, 'Amen', and the elders fell down
and worshipped. (Revelation 5:12-14)

Questions to Consider:

1) In what way is the Rest we now have through the Gospel a foretaste of the Everlasting Rest we long for?

2) Why is it important not to confuse what we have now with what we will have then? What are the dangers of seeking ultimate fulfillment in this present world?

3) How is it possible to live for the Glory of God and our true Rest and happiness at the same time?

Chapter Three

Before We Proceed

Friends, I know I am moving slowly. You might be wanting me to dive right in and get on to talking about Heaven. I fully understand! I want to talk about Heaven too!

But first things first. (We do all want "instant" everything these days... but some things we cannot rush!) I need to lay a good foundation and present some vital presuppositions, without which we cannot proceed.

So, open your heart to the Lord, and your mind to His Word and my simple book, and let's explore non-negotiable presuppositions to God's Rest.

1) *This Rest assumes weariness.* It is for those who have tried and failed. It is a haven for the broken and a harbour for the storm-tossed. It is for sinners. It is for those who have learned they cannot help themselves. It is for those who are tired of sin, tired of rebelling, tired of trying to establish their own righteousness, tired of religion. It is for those who have given up and have cast themselves, for life and for death, upon Jesus. It is for the sin-worn prodigal and for the pleasure-worn rich man. It is for the down and out and the up and out.

> *For the Son of Man came to seek and to save the lost.*
> (Luke 19:10)

But the tax collector stood at a distance. He would not even look up to heaven, but beat his breast and said, "God, have mercy on me, a sinner."

I tell you that this man, rather than the other, went home justified before God. For all those who exalt themselves will be humbled, and those who humble themselves will be exalted. (Luke 18:13,14)

Come to me, all you who are weary and burdened, and I will give you rest. Take my yoke upon you and learn from me, for I am gentle and humble in heart, and you will find rest for your souls. For my yoke is easy and my burden is light. (Matthew 11:28-30)

2) *This journey of discovery assumes that the end and goal of the journey is happiness in God Himself.* If you have any other goal (prosperity, health, fame, ease, earthly comfort) your journey is wrong from the start. We are assuming that you are seeking true Rest. The angels and believers now in glory have it, demons and the damned are beyond hope of it. Their sin was to begin the entire journey wrongly – by making anything besides God Himself their goal. So, the very first step along the way is choosing God as our treasure and happiness.

> *Take delight in the Lord,*
> *and he will give you the desires of your heart.*
> (Psalm 37:4)

3) *Our journey towards Rest assumes we are now separated and distanced from God.* Our sins have separated us from our God.

> *But your iniquities have separated you from your God ...*
> (Isaiah 59:2)

All people are headed somewhere. No one is standing still. The issue is one of direction, not of motion. The man who appears to be the laziest of all may be in fact speeding his way toward Hell. The fact of moving assumes a distance from our goal.

If a person does not know he is separated from God, he will never stop, and turn, and move in a new direction. A lost man who does not know he is lost does not bother to retrace his steps. A man who is unaware that he has lost his money does not know to look for it. Who travels when he thinks he has already arrived? A person with a true hope of Heaven begins by realizing that he is far off. He is not only separated, but he *knows it.* The tragic reality with so many is that they have lost their God, their souls, and their way, and are oblivious to it. Or, if they do know it, they will not admit it. They will despise and ridicule the one who tries to alert them.

Every one of us is distanced from God because of sin. Even if we think we are only separated from earthly happiness and pleasures, the real separation is from God. What sin has confused is the direction of our journey, not the fact of it. It is only when God the Holy Spirit arrests us with the Gospel, stops us, turns us around in repentance, and gives us grace to take that first step in a new direction that our journey toward Rest begins.

4) *It is assumed that there is a meaningful understanding of what our Rest will be like.* There is at least a glimpse of the beauty of God and the wonders of Heaven. We cannot make something our goal if we know nothing about it. The athlete has at least some knowledge of the glory for which he is training. The treasure hunter has at least some understanding of the wonders for which he searches. We are not wandering about aimlessly. We are not groping in the dark. We have heard reports of something more wonderful than anything else. We have caught a glimpse of a glory that outshines anything we can see here. Otherwise we would never set our course.

They must turn from evil and do good; they must seek peace and pursue it.
(1 Peter 3:11)

5) But! Before we can even begin our journey toward this Rest, *there must be something Greater, outside of ourselves, to get us moving.* We are naturally dead in sin, stuck fast in the pit of guilt, and incapable of moving on our own. Just like a watch, even if finely made, is motionless unless someone winds its spring, so we, even though we are the image bearers of God, are incapable of even starting to move toward Rest unless God moves us first.

This whole discovery presupposes the grace of God moving first upon us.

No one can come to me unless the Father who sent me draws them, and I will raise them up at the last day.
(John 6:44)

Even once started, be careful that you do not begin to trust yourself while on your journey to Heaven. The entire Christian life is by the grace and power which God alone supplies. Stay dependent upon God the entire way. Do not take anything for granted, but humble yourself daily, moment by moment, believing God alone to be your strength and supply for your journey to His wonderful Rest. Jesus is there at the beginning to get us going, and He is there all along the way to keep us going!

... looking unto Jesus the author and finisher of our faith...
(Hebrews 12:2 KJV)

6) *We are not passive in our journey to our Rest.* Now, God moves us not like we might move a stone. A stone is lifeless and totally passive. We are not lifeless and passive in our trip to Heaven. Yes, we are submitted to God; yes, He is the first mover and continual source of our strength, but no, we are not just along for the ride! While I am not sure if anyone can rightly explain the nature of the life of God within us, what is vital is that we understand that in some way God Himself infuses, or fills, or transforms us so that we might cooperate with Him in this adventure of faith.

> *... that Christ may dwell in your hearts through faith ...*
> (Ephesians 1:17)

We will Rest one day, but we must move today! I am not in any way saying that you can earn your way to Heaven. But I am stating again that Christianity is not experienced on the sofa but on the race-track (Hebrews 12:1), the battlefield (Psalm 144:1), and the wrestling mat (Ephesians 6:10ff). Sitting still will endanger your journey toward Heaven as surely (and perhaps more deceptively) as running away from it. True, when we have done our very best, we are just "unprofitable servants," (Luke 17:10) but the answer is not to be the lazy servant who hides his talents in the sand.

7) *We also must be sure that our direction and our strides are on the right road*! Not all roads lead to Heaven (as fashionable as it is today to assert so.) God, in His infinite mercy, has made *a* Way, a sure and certain Way. What a merciful God we have! God was under no obligation to make *any* way, and having desired to do so, was under no obligation to make more than *one* way. Be careful that you do not think yourself to be wiser and more merciful than God in inventing your own way, or insisting that other ways must be just as valid as the way of Jesus. God has decreed that Jesus Christ is the Door – the *only*

Door. And He has ordained that faith in Jesus is the Key – the *only* Key - that will open that Door.

Jesus answered, 'I am the way and the truth and the life. No one comes to the Father except through me.'
(John 14:6)

As God has graciously designed that Jesus Christ is the only way of salvation, and that faith in Jesus Christ is the only way to God, there is to be a conscious, deliberate, focused faith in Jesus, not just some vague notion or foggy idea. Jesus is the Way to Heaven, faith is the way to Jesus, and walking in obedience is the way of faith.

Salvation is found in no one else, for there is no other name under heaven given to mankind by which we must be saved.
(Acts 4:12)

8) *Moving in the right direction will not get you to your Rest if you do not keep going*! You cannot keep going unless you put effort into your journey. A lazy person will not finish the course! Again, I am not in any way suggesting that it is our sweating to keep the Law, our own religious efforts that will save us! But I am saying that we must follow hard after Jesus. The sloth will find one day that he has yawned himself into a dark eternity. What a cost: laziness in exchange for his soul! Listen, there has never been a holy person who has said, "I have been too diligent with my soul. I have read the Bible too much. I have over-prayed. I have repented more than I should have." No one has ever been sorry for diligence and constancy in his Christian life.

You will be hated by everyone because of me, but the one who stands firm to the end will be saved.

17

(Matthew 10:22)

If the journey to our Rest is as easy as our generation imagines and insists upon, then Jesus and His first followers did not know what they were talking about. If someone has gotten to Heaven through the popular, lazy, pseudo-Christianity all around us, then there must be another way not known to God and His Word.

God knows the Way better than we do, and His Word is a sure light for the road.

Not that I have already obtained all this, or have already arrived at my goal, but I press on to take hold of that for which Christ Jesus took hold of me. Brothers and sisters, I do not consider myself yet to have taken hold of it. But one thing I do: forgetting what is behind and straining towards what is ahead, I press on towards the goal to win the prize for which God has called me heavenwards in Christ Jesus. (Philippians 3:12-14)

9) *He will give all strength to the weary and all power to persevere.* Do not be afraid that you will be too weak to run this race!

> *He gives strength to the weary*
> *and increases the power of the weak.*
> *Even youths grow tired and weary,*
> *and young men stumble and fall;*
> *but those who hope in the Lord*
> *will renew their strength.*
> *They will soar on wings like eagles;*
> *they will run and not grow weary,*
> *they will walk and not be faint.*
> (Isaiah 40:29-31)

Again I can hear some saying, "You are trying to make us work our way to Heaven!" "Do you think we can add to Jesus' work for us on the Cross?" "You are turning our Jesus into half a Saviour, with ourselves being the other half!" We need to be very clear here: Our duty to Jesus is very different from our duty to the Law. Before we trusted in Jesus, our efforts to gain Heaven by "being good enough" were nothing but self-righteous legalism (Philippians 3:7-9). Our duty to Jesus is to give up all reliance upon ourselves and trust only and wholly in Him. He has paid the entire price for our salvation. We add nothing to it. But that does not mean that we can snooze our way into Heaven! Our response to Him is to receive Him, turn away from sin (repentance is a life-long Christian action), deny ourselves, be willing to suffer for Him, and doubtless go through many, many trials – all the while counting it all joy because we are in fellowship with Jesus!

Again, *all* of our righteousness is in Jesus, none in ourselves. We offer no righteousness for our salvation. But, having trusted in Christ, we are empowered by His Holy Spirit to live and watch and war and run and wrestle and keep going. Our "doing" cannot gain Heaven without Jesus, but Jesus saves us and empowers us for "doing" His will.

Therefore, my dear friends, as you have always obeyed – not only in my presence, but now much more in my absence – continue to work out your salvation with fear and trembling, for it is God who works in you to will and to act in order to fulfil his good purpose. (Philippians 2:12,13)

... so that you may live a life worthy of the Lord and please him in every way: bearing fruit in every good work, growing in the knowledge of God, being strengthened with all power according to his glorious might so that you may have great endurance and

patience, and giving joyful thanks to the Father, who has qualified you to share in the inheritance of his holy people in the kingdom of light. (Colossians 1:10-12)

The fact that God is faithful over us, and that Jesus will lose none of all that His Father has given to Him (John 6:39), does not make this encouragement to persevere and this warning against laziness useless. We never outgrow the need to be constantly pointed away from ourselves and from our bent toward self-righteousness, back to Jesus and our calling to Him alone. Just as the Galatians began in the Spirit then tried to finish in their own efforts, and just as the Corinthians first rejoiced in the simplicity of Christ but then became enchanted by all sorts of sin and fanaticism, so we, even the "best" of us, can take our eyes off of Jesus, becoming worldly, legalistic, or indolent. Our "duty" (sweet duty!) is to remain close to Jesus at all costs.

I am the vine; you are the branches. If you remain in me and I in you, you will bear much fruit; apart from me you can do nothing.
(John 15:5)

10) *It is assumed that you have a true and strong desire to Rest.* There will be no half-hearted who gain Heaven. Why would you even want to be there if your heart was not set there? Think of it this way: Your heart must go to Heaven before your body does.

Whom have I in heaven but you?
And earth has nothing I desire besides you.
My flesh and my heart may fail,
but God is the strength of my heart
and my portion for ever.
(Psalm 73:25,26)

Since, then, you have been raised with Christ, set your hearts on things above, where Christ is, seated at the right hand of God. Set your minds on things above, not on earthly things. For you died, and your life is now hidden with Christ in God. (Colossians 3:1-3)

If you would rather have Jesus above all else, then you will have Jesus! But if you would rather something else above Him, then that thing is sure to be yours. Remember when Jesus looked in love upon the rich young man and urged him to part with his idol of money to gain Life (Mark 10:17ff)? That young man - right then and there - made a choice and walked away. He made a sad choice, but a choice: He placed wealth over Christ, and he got it ... at the expense of Jesus. Like him, we too are so often more passionate about lesser things than we are of Jesus. What remains of our "old nature" might give us a weaker desire for lesser things, but that desire still remains. We need to examine our hearts!

11) Finally, *we must know from the start that this journey to Rest is marked by trials and troubles.* Yes, Jesus has delivered us from the burden of religion and religious works, but not from the trials that come with following Him. Do not let this put you off the endeavor! But know that Jesus Himself promised no less: "In the world ye shall have tribulation." What an honest Saviour! "But be of good cheer, I have overcome the world" (John 16:33 KJV). What a triumphant Saviour!

These trials are not because Jesus is unfaithful, but because the world is evil. Jesus' yoke is easy, Jesus' burden is light (Matthew 11:28-30). The problem is not with Him, but with our own weaknesses and wrong desires. Add to them a real enemy who works to destroy and discourage, add the fact that we live in a sinful, rebellious world, and we have a recipe for a war! At our best, we are all weak and feeble followers. If you never find yourself struggling while on your way to Heaven, that is not a good sign, but a danger sign that you are not even headed there. If you are not battling, be warned! You might have made peace with your sinful self, this fallen world, and your devilish enemy.

Bearing all the above in mind, a follower of Jesus must determine with all his heart to walk this walk, to take this road, to fight this fight, to pursue this prize. God's part is sure; attend to yours. God is ready to get you safely to Himself, to see to it that you will not lose your reward.

We do ourselves great harm when we worry more about God's faithfulness than our own, as though His heart is more suspect than ours! Saving grace in a soul is proven in a life given to trusting and following Jesus through thick and thin - and even persecution - until Rest is gained.

I have told you these things, so that in me you may have peace. In this world you will have trouble. But take heart! I have overcome the world. (John 16:33)

The Rest is glorious, God is faithful, Jesus' blood is enough, and God's promise is sure. Don't be afraid of missing Heaven because there is something lacking in these. If you fear anything, fear that you will look away when you should look to Jesus, get distracted by this world when you should be yearning for the next, love your sin when you should love godliness, be sleeping when you should be awake, be at ease when you should be at war.

Scriptures to Ponder:

Therefore, since the promise of entering his rest still stands, let us be careful that none of you be found to have fallen short of it.(Hebrews 4:1)

Through these he has given us his very great and precious promises, so that through them you may participate in the divine nature, having escaped the corruption in the world caused by evil desires.
For this very reason, make every effort to add to your faith goodness; and to goodness, knowledge; and to knowledge, self-control; and to self-control, perseverance; and to perseverance, godliness; and to godliness, mutual affection; and to mutual affection, love. For if you possess these qualities in increasing measure, they will keep you from being ineffective and unproductive in your knowledge of our Lord Jesus Christ. But whoever does not have them is short-sighted and blind, forgetting that they have been cleansed from their past sins.
(2 Peter 1:4-9)

No, I strike a blow to my body and make it my slave so that after I have preached to others, I myself will not be disqualified for the prize. (1 Corinthians 9:27)

May God himself, the God of peace, sanctify you through and through. May your whole spirit, soul and body be kept blameless at the coming of our Lord Jesus Christ. The one who calls you is faithful, and he will do it. (1 Thessalonians 5:23,24)

To him who is able to keep you from stumbling and to present you before his glorious presence without fault and with great joy – to the only God our Saviour be glory, majesty, power and authority, through Jesus Christ our Lord, before all ages, now and for evermore! Amen. (Jude 24,25)

Questions to Consider:

1) What are the differences between trying to save ourselves by our own efforts and following Jesus with all our hearts?

2) How do we embrace both the promises of God to keep us and the warnings from God? Are the warnings a part of the keeping?

3) If Jesus' burden is light, and if His commands are not burdensome, why is the Journey sometimes so hard? Is the problem found in God and the Gospel or elsewhere?

Chapter Four

Understanding This Rest

We are barely on the front porch of the mansion we call Heaven. We are standing on the first step of the outer court – dare we try to take a look behind the curtain?

Who am *I* to try to teach you about such wonderful things? What do *I* know? But! If I wait until I know all, I will never speak at all. Just because we cannot yet know all things fully does not mean we cannot now know some things truly. There are things God has graciously given us to know even now!

The secret things belong to the Lord our God, but the things revealed belong to us and to our children forever, that we may follow all the words of this law. (Deuteronomy 29:29)

We have the Bible, and the help of His Holy Spirit, so may the Lord graciously show us something of the wonderful things He has in store for us. May we catch a glimpse of the prize for which we will happily give up all lesser things. May we see even a little of the glory that is ahead for us that we might joyfully live for Jesus and willingly suffer when our following demands it.

The kingdom of heaven is like treasure hidden in a field. When a man found it, he hid it again, and then in his joy went and sold all he had and bought that field. (Matthew 13:44)

But Stephen, full of the Holy Spirit, looked up to heaven and saw the glory of God, and Jesus standing at the right hand of

God. 'Look,' he said, 'I see heaven open and the Son of Man standing at the right hand of God.' (Acts 7:55,56)

Let's glimpse behind the curtain:

1) *Rest speaks of the end of a journey, or a labour completed, or a goal reached.* All we know and use now to help us on our way will no longer be needed when we are at our Rest. These things, so vital now, will be not needed then. Good things: prayer, preaching, sacraments, fasting, weeping, watching against sin and temptation, will be of the past! Prophesying, tongues, imperfect knowledge, all necessary here, will not be needed there. Faith will be replaced by sight! The unbeliever will be past hope, and the believer past fear. We will learn and grow without the hindrance caused by the sin and weakness that hinders us now. Wearisome toil for temporary necessities will not be there. No more exhausting ourselves for what does not last!

2) *The Rest that is ahead offers us an absence from every evil thing in every form.* We have grown used to evil as our constant companion in this life, but not there. At the gates of Heaven we will say a happy "goodbye" to the sin and weeping which has followed us every day here. Just as God in Himself will not abide sin now, so in His Heaven He will have none of it - forever. Grief and sorrow will be gone. Weak, feeble bodies, aches and pains, disabled children and decrepit elderly ... all these will be redeemed, healed, and whole! Fears that grip us now will be gone. No more joy-robbing worries. Groans and sighs will be no more. No more hospitals, ambulances or cemeteries. Yes, we now weep while the world rejoices, but our weeping will be turned to joy, and no one will ever be able to rob us of it.

Does this sound too fanciful for you? Too good to be true? Listen, God is not the True, Good, and Perfect God the Bible tells us He is if His Heaven is not the full flower and fruit of all that is Good, with absolutely no trace of evil.

And I heard a loud voice from the throne saying, 'Look! God's dwelling-place is now among the people, and he will dwell with them. They will be his people, and God himself will be with them and be their God. He will wipe every tear from their eyes. There will be no more death or mourning or crying or pain, for the old order of things has passed away. (Revelation 21:3,4)

> *And a highway will be there;*
> *it will be called the Way of Holiness;*
> *it will be for those who walk on that Way.*
> *The unclean will not journey on it;*
> *wicked fools will not go about on it.*
> *No lion will be there,*
> *nor any ravenous beast;*
> *they will not be found there.*
> *But only the redeemed will walk there.*
> (Isaiah 35:8,9)

3) *In our Rest we will be the owners of brand-new, glorified bodies.* Our present fallen bodies can never embrace the full glories of heaven. Not just our souls, but our bodies as well will be glorified and therefore able to embrace all that God is and has for us. Here and now:

> *... no eye has seen,*
> *... no ear has heard,*
> *and ... no human mind has conceived –*
> *the things God has prepared for those who love him.*
> (1 Corinthians 2:9)

27

But then and there:

*... the power that enables him to bring everything under his
control, will transform our lowly bodies so that they will be like
his glorious body.*
(Philippians 3:21)

Made to be like Him! Glorified! How else could we fully enjoy
God and all He has prepared for us? Our sight –now dim - then
able to delight in beauty, *His* Beauty, like never before. Our
taste buds – dull here - there able to enjoy flavours beyond
anything known below.   Our hearing – muted now - then
hearing the beauties of music as never heard in this life. Ahead
are deeper joys, higher glories than the best this present world
can give to us.

4) But, all these bow to the greatest wonder of our Rest:
knowing God in unending, unfolding, ever-growing fullness.
Please do not be surprised that I do not have the words to
express the wonders of knowing and beholding God, Father,
Son, and Holy Spirit as we will in that Day. If John, the disciple
so especially loved by Jesus, could barely express the wonders
of Heaven and the New Jerusalem; if Paul could not speak of
the things he saw in his vision of the highest Heaven, then who
am I to speak of these things? I barely know my own soul, how
can I – in this life – but barely know God in His Infinite
Majesty? How can I really understand now what it will be like
to exist then as a glorified person? We will never be able to
embrace such wonders until we are encompassed by them. As
the blind can hear of light and colours but not really imagine
them, or the deaf might read about music but not be able to
conceive of it, so we presently lack the ability to know God as
we will be able to in our eternal Rest.

For now we see only a reflection as in a mirror; then we shall see face to face. Now I know in part; then I shall know fully, even as I am fully known. (1 Corinthians 13:12)

And God raised us up with Christ and seated us with him in the heavenly realms in Christ Jesus, in order that in the coming ages he might show the incomparable riches of his grace, expressed in his kindness to us in Christ Jesus. (Ephesians 2:6,7)

I tower over an ant hill and see them all hurrying about their business, oblivious to me, my nature, and my ways. Yet I, like them, am but a creature, a vapour. How much greater the distance between myself and the uncreated, Eternal God! Thanks to God making Himself known in creation, in Christ, and His Word, we do have now a true knowledge of Him, but how small and dim it is compared to what it will be! We have now a glimpse; then we will behold in fullness.

All good, beauty, knowledge, and joy find their source in God, the Father, the Son, the Holy Spirit. Any of these found in us now are but a drop in the vast ocean of God's wonderful nature. But what is now a drop will one day be overflowing fullness! However much grace and glory you have experienced so far, there is more – *much more* - to come. Think of the hope for future joy and fullness found in this one sentence from the Lord Jesus:

Father, I want those you have given me to be with me where I am, and to see my glory, the glory you have given me because you loved me before the creation of the world. (John 17:24)

I would not take the whole world for that one Bible verse! Every word is packed with joy, goodness, and hope.

One day we will eat of the Tree of Life in the Paradise of God (Revelation 2:7). Think: If the Lord has already given us here and now more joy than the richest of this world can know (Psalm 4:7), what will our joy be like when we are living in the eternal daylight of God's Heaven? In that Day He will fulfill our joy with the very smile on His face.

This blessedness that believers in Jesus are now beginning to taste and will one day feast upon is higher than anything else known in creation. For this, and nothing less, we were created, have been redeemed, and are destined! If the Bible did not tell us of it, we would never imagine it or believe in it. But this is the Hope for the person the Lord delights to honour: joy unspeakable in His presence forever:

> *Thou wilt shew me the path of life: in thy presence*
> *is fulness of joy; at thy right hand there are pleasures for*
> *evermore.*
> (Psalm 16:11 KJV)

Believer! If the sun, moon, and stars praise Him, if the animals and senseless creatures are called upon to praise and honour the Lord, then how much more should *we*, those made in His image and redeemed by His blood, praise Him *now* in joyful anticipation of *then*? Yes, all His works praise Him, but we who have been redeemed from sin and death certainly must praise Him most of all.

There are troubles and trials during this journey! Oh, how often this side of Heaven do we cry out to God! At times it seems as if God is beyond the range of our cry and does not hear, or the clouds between us and Heaven are too dense to allow even our loudest cries to reach Him. Sometimes we get angry at what seems to be such a great canyon between God and us. We can even wish that death would remember its job and get on with it! "When will I be near God and far from sin?" My dear friend, take courage and rejoice. The day is close at hand when you will be in the very presence of God. All that you have desired will be fulfilled in Him. We shall live with Him as cherished members of his family. How we need to remember this today when sin tries to enchant us!

Better is one day in your courts than a thousand elsewhere; I would rather be a doorkeeper in the house of my God than dwell in the tents of the wicked.
(Psalm 84:10)

Our future hope needs to be enough for us today. We will, one day very soon, literally dwell in His presence, around His throne, we His children, He our Father, one with His Son, who is one with His Father.

Can there be more? There is!

5) *Our Rest will find us so transformed that all of our abilities and powers shall come to the fullness that God has intended.* In our Rest we will not be like a stone or some other dead object when it is at rest. Our Rest is not a cessation of all action. Like the raw ore which hides the pure gold, so our lives here and now hide something vastly more wonderful than we can now conceive. The change from ore to gold is nothing close to the change from these bodies of death to our glorified bodies. Think about this: If *grace* has done such a transforming work in us here and now, so that we can truly say, "I am not the person I used to be, I have been born again!" then what will *glory* accomplish in us?

So will it be with the resurrection of the dead. The body that is sown is perishable, it is raised imperishable; it is sown in

31

dishonour, it is raised in glory; it is sown in weakness, it is raised in power; it is sown a natural body, it is raised a spiritual body. (1 Corinthians 15:42-44)

Think: All of our strengths and senses will be glorified. Eyes, ears, minds, our entire bodies. We might then say "I have eyes and hands and I hear and taste, but it is not what I once had! Everything is ... *wonderful* (glorified, intensified)!" These frail, tiresome lumps we call our bodies will - in their glory – exceed the sun in its glory! And, without a doubt, as God will glorify our senses and strengths, He will enlarge our ability to enjoy and rejoice in our glorified bodies.

And those he predestined, he also called; those he called, he also justified; those he justified, he also glorified. (Romans 8:30)

Will you be bored in the eternal presence of God? Not for a moment! Your glorified capacities will enable you to understand, and enjoy, and praise, and worship God and all that He is into all eternity. Our minds will be expanded, and then filled, with a right knowledge of Him. Our hearts will be enlarged, and then overflow, with a right love for Him. I know we cannot really grasp this now. Of course we cannot. We are tainted by sin, and distraction, and worldliness. As a rock cannot imagine itself as gold, so it is impossible for us to imagine – when we look at our present selves - what we will then be. Even so, we need to embrace this as our destiny in Jesus and begin *now*, even in our feeble ways, to learn and do what we will do *then* in our renewed bodies: praise and worship our wonderful God.

Now think about this: both our bodies *and* our spirits glorified! Our whole being, our entire nature, made able to know love and enjoy God beyond anything we can imagine here and now.

Just like our bodily senses will be enabled to taste, see, hear, move, and serve with power that we cannot fathom, so our spiritual senses will be able to know, praise, think, love, and enjoy in unimaginable ways - to the rich enjoyment of our entire being.

What a motive to deny self now, to fight sin today, to resist Satan every hour, to turn from worldliness moment by moment!

To know about things of this present life is considered a great prize. And so it should be. Knowledge is a wonderful thing. We spend our lives learning about what we can currently see and feel and touch. We can plot the planets in their orbits and discover the ways of the smallest cells. But! If knowing the marvels of creation is wonderful, how much greater will it be to know the wonders of our Creator! We are created with the capacity to know, love, and enjoy *God*. We can know a little bit here, but – then – unimaginable wonders will be ours to know.

God *wants* to be known. He wants His wonders to be known. He is not playing hide-and-seek with us. He has put within us the capacity to know, and a natural bent to want to know Truth, that is, Himself. God has wired us in such a way that we *cannot* be finally satisfied with anything lower as our goal (try as we may), but only with Himself, in whom reside all the riches of Beauty, Knowledge, and Truth.

> *He has made everything beautiful in its time.*
> *He has also set eternity in the human heart ...*
> (Ecclesiastes 3:11)

> *... that [we] may know Christ, in whom are hidden all the*
> *mysteries of wisdom and knowledge.* (Colossians 2:3)

33

A truly studious and knowledge-hungry person knows the sweet connection between searching and discovery. But the Christian knows a still sweeter connection between the search for higher truth and its discovery. Listen: A believer, with an open Bible and an open heart begins *now* to discover an open Heaven! The curtain is drawn back and he sees, for a moment, even dimly, a glimpse of Jesus. Just as a momentary glance at the sun in all its brilliance dazzles the eyes so as to make everything else seem colourless and dim, so catching a glimpse of something ever brighter, the Son of God, makes things - all things which usually fascinate us - seem dull and dark by comparison. This is especially true for those who suffer for Jesus: How bright He then shines, and how dull the world then becomes!

Christian! Whatever we have known of God here, however wonderful our experience now, it is nothing compared to what we will one day know of Him! Here we are seeing through a glass darkly, but one day we will see face to face! The difference between what we know now and will know then is as vast as the difference between our perishable bodies here and our imperishable bodies there, or as distant as a seed is from the full flower.

What is so wonderful about Heaven is that we will know God in unhindered Truth. It would not be Heaven otherwise. Eternal Life is knowing God. Without God, not just present, but experienced and known, Heaven would not be worth inhabiting:

Now this is eternal life: that they know you, the only true God,
and Jesus Christ, whom you have sent.
(John 17:3)

If we are so caught up into Jesus in Heaven, will we have any use or reason *then* to remember *now*? Will we have any remembrance of our past earthly pilgrimage when we are present with the Lord in Glory? I think so. Why? Perhaps to help us value the wonders of what the Gospel has bought us. Remember, our knowledge will be enlarged, not diminished. So I doubt that the knowledge of the past will be taken away. Ah! But our past will not be remembered to condemn us, but to bring us to a true place of embracing the cost at which we were redeemed. "I was saved from all *that*?" Here, we do not really appreciate the depth of sin from which Jesus has saved us. There we will ... all to the praise of Jesus and the thrill of our souls. Like Moses on the mountain, to be able to see both the wilderness past and the land of promise ahead, to be able from Heaven to see history, and to compare the two, will bring us to a new and magnified appreciation of just what it means to be saved: "No wonder this cost the dear Son of God His very blood to save me!" "Look where faith has brought me!" "See what the Holy Spirit's work has accomplished for me!" "The winds of grace have guided me to a wonderful harbour!" "Soul! Be ashamed that you ever questioned the goodness of God that guided you here, that you dared to question *His* care instead of *your* foolishness." "How could I have ever questioned for a moment the wonder of Jesus' love, or pushed against the work of God's Spirit?"

Perhaps then we will be ashamed of all the times and ways we thought God's dealings with us were unfair, unloving, or too hard. Then we will see that the ways we thought were hard were needful. We will see that special fruit was being grown in the valleys; that the bitter tears of this brief life were in fact producing sweet wine for the next. It will be in looking back that we will see that the Lord had sweeter plans for us than we ever dreamed, and that all His workings for us were necessary.

We will be assured then that His saving work was as certain when He broke us as when He mended us.

As the memory of the wicked will torment them into eternity – grace ignored, situations wasted, the Gospel approaches of a good God rejected – so will the memory of the redeemed sweeten their joys into eternity.

6) *At last our hearts will be full of love for God.* You will know, if you are truly a believer in Jesus, what every dear saint knows: The coldness of your own heart toward God. How we wish we could love Jesus more! I cannot but want to love Him, (He is so wonderful) but so often my heart lets my desire to love Him down. Be encouraged, believer. Our salvation is not finished yet! Yes, we are pardoned; yes, we are justified; but we are still imperfect in love. The day is coming ... it *really* is ... when we will be perfected in love and filled to the full measure with the love of God. Even now, when we consider God's past mercies our cold hearts are warmed. Thinking about His kindnesses to us begins to awaken fires within our dormant hearts. But when we know Him more we will love Him more. When we see the fullness of our forgiveness we will love the Forgiver in fullness. The day is coming soon when we will be immersed in the delights of His love and totally content in all that He is. Love for God that we (so it seems) so often have to work for in this life shall be our *undeserved* reward in the next!

I have made you known to them, and will continue to make you known in order that the love you have for me may be in them, and I myself may be in them.
(John 17:26)

And so we know and rely on the love God has for us. God is love. Whoever lives in love lives in God, and God in them.
(1 John 4:16)

But there is more: It is not enough that we will one day fully love as we are loved, but is it not amazing that God will even allow us to love Him? Arms that have embraced sin, hearts that have hated good, lips that have spoken perversely; *He* allows *us* to love *Him*? And, even more again, when we love with perfect hearts, we will not in any way love as fully as we are loved. Do not think that you can ever out-love God! The Son of God, who opened His arms for you on a cross, and His heart with a spear, this Jesus, who loved you when you hated Him, when you even hated yourself, if He so proved His love for you *then*, how much more *now* that you have drawn near by faith, been made His child by grace, and have returned at least some love for His great love? And then, how much more when grace has finished its redeeming work and you are presented to Him as His spotless bride?

I hope (how I hope!) that we do not consider the love of God too lightly, but I'm afraid that we do! *God* loves *us*! We need to think on this, walk around it, explore it from every angle, until we are *affected* by it. We are, and forever will be, embraced by Eternal Arms in Eternal Love. And this love is not just some idea or wispy feeling. It came from Heaven to earth. It went from earth to a cross, and then to a grave ... and then to glory. It was weary. It wept. It knew temptation and hunger. This love fasted, prayed, healed, taught, and thirsted. It was scorned and scourged, spat upon and beaten. Finally, it was crucified and pierced. This is the love that embraces us!

But God demonstrates his own love for us in this: while we were still sinners, Christ died for us.
(Romans 5:8)

37

When our creature love, one day made complete, meets His Creator Love, what a wonderful day that will be! But even now, imperfect though we are, Jesus' love is constant, unchanging, and perfect. His love is the magnet that draws our hearts, and His now perfect love is the love with which our now imperfect love dances.

Our Rest will be in the fullness of this love. No wonder the very angels long to look into these things! But only we who have rebelled and deserve wrath will experience the full wonders of redemptive love. His Infinite Love must of necessity be a mystery to be embraced, even while it cannot to be fully understood, by our finite minds. But, while we cannot grasp it all, may we join with our fellow Jesus followers in knowing all that we can of the height, and breadth, and length and depth of the Love of God in Jesus Christ (Ephesians 3:18).

The fullness of our Rest will be experienced in the fullness of our joy. This journey is heading to a *joyous* destination, where in loving and being beloved of God, we who have trusted and followed Jesus will know a joy unimagined now. (I wonder, could this gift of joy be the "white stone" spoken of in Revelation 2:17?) Certainly this joy will be beyond the reach of any thief and any time-bound discouragement.

All of Jesus' providential leadings and guidings are bringing us to this Joy-filled Rest. *He* wept and suffered that *we* might be full of joy! If even now He wants His joy in us (John 15:11); if even now He gives His Holy Spirit to comfort us, His promises to cheer us, and shows us something of our future happiness; if even now He gives us endless and abundant grace, leads us to green pastures and still waters, and opens up fountains of living waters; if even now He assures us that our present sufferings are contributing to a future unspeakable joy and that His disciplines now are shaping us that we might enjoy our future Rest ... if He does all this for our *present* joy, what will be the experience of our *future* joy?

7) *We will be overflowing with unspeakable joy.* What a place of joy Heaven will be! There we, being perfectly fitted to hold all the joy that Jesus can give us, will find our "jobs" to be the business of forever rejoicing in God. Perhaps now you long for joy. Your life has been hard ... harder than most. Here you pray, wait, and yearn. Listen! Joy is ahead for you! All that you can hold! More than you ever imagined you could have! More than your heart ever desired! So for now, in this pilgrim's way, keep your eyes on Jesus and your feet from sinful paths, trusting God to measure out His joy to you as He knows is best, being always more concerned for your eternal safety than your present ease.

8) But we are not finished yet. There is still more: *Heaven's Joy over Us.* This superabundance of joy will not be yours alone to enjoy. All of Heaven will rejoice with you. If the angels exploded with joy at your conversion, what will they do at your glorification? They will welcome you and celebrate your safe arrival home. And then Jesus! Seeing the reward of His sufferings in your homecoming, He will rejoice in the completion of what He promised His Father: losing *none* of *all* that His Father had given to Him for safekeeping (John 6:39), including *you.* We are now the seed, then the harvested fruit of his labours, in whom He will be glorified and His Father forever honoured. On that day all creation will know that His sufferings were not in vain, and He will rejoice over His blood-bought inheritance, and we shall rejoice in Him:

Both the one who makes people holy and those who are made holy are of the same family. So Jesus is not ashamed to call them brothers and sisters.

39

He says, 'I will declare your name to my brothers and sisters;
in the assembly I will sing your praises.'

And again, ... 'Here am I, and the children God has given me.'
(Hebrews 2:11-13)

But it will not stop with the angels, or with Jesus, but so will the Father rejoice at your joy. So often we have grieved His Spirit and broken His Father heart. Yet He has patiently waited and watched, ever searching for us prodigals to return, always celebrating our arrival. If that is how He rejoices now, how much more will He rejoice then, when our arrival is final, and our wanderings are forever over! His joys now at our frequent returnings are but shadows of His joy at our final home-coming.

This Rest will not only be ours, but His! If His seventh-day Sabbath celebrates a finished and "good" present creation, what will His Eternal Sabbath be but an infinitely greater celebration of a finished work of redemption, preservation, glorification, and new creation? "Good" indeed!

The Bible tells us that God takes delight in His redeemed people. That means you and me! Believe it today in anticipation of that Perfect Day!

Write these words in letters of gold on your heart:

The Lord thy God in the midst of thee is mighty; he will save, he
will rejoice over thee with joy; he will rest in his love, he will joy
over thee with singing.
(Zepheniah 3:17 KJV)

Scriptures to Rejoice In:

I have told you this so that my joy may be in you and that your joy may be complete ... I say these things while I am still in the world, so that they may have the full measure of my joy within them. (John 15:11; 17:13)

And I pray that you, being rooted and established in love, may have power, together with all the Lord's holy people, to grasp how wide and long and high and deep is the love of Christ, and to know this love that surpasses knowledge – that you may be filled to the measure of all the fullness of God.
(Ephesians 3:17-19)

I have made you known to them, and will continue to make you known in order that the love you have for me may be in them and that I myself may be in them.
(John 17:26)

After this I looked, and there before me was a great multitude that no one could count, from every nation, tribe, people and language, standing before the throne and before the Lamb. They were wearing white robes and were holding palm branches in their hands. And they cried out in a loud voice:
'Salvation belongs to our God,
who sits on the throne,
and to the Lamb.'
All the angels were standing round the throne and round the elders and the four living creatures. They fell down on their faces before the throne and worshipped God, saying:
'Amen!
Praise and glory
and wisdom and thanks and honour
and power and strength

41

be to our God for ever and ever.
Amen!'
(Revelation 7:10-12)

Questions to Consider:

1) How can the consideration of a wonderful Heaven strengthen us for valiant living for Jesus today?

2) Considering the coldness of our love here, how does considering the warmth of Jesus' love for us now, and the promise of our full love for Him one day, encourage us today?

3) Have you ever thought about what *God* gets out of your salvation? His Joy in your joy? What does this discovery mean to you?

Chapter Five

Four Foundations of Our Rest

We have drawn back the curtain just a little. Through the Gospel window we have caught a glimpse of what is otherwise unknowable. Dare we proceed? Will we find a willing God and an open Heaven? Or, having been banished once from Paradise, will we find still a flaming sword?

The Bible encourages us to venture forward in faith, being sure of God's willingness to welcome us through Jesus Christ:

Therefore, brothers and sisters, since we have confidence to enter the Most Holy Place by the blood of Jesus, by a new and living way opened for us through the curtain, that is, his body,
And having an high priest over the house of God; Let us draw near with a true heart in full assurance of faith, having our hearts sprinkled from an evil conscience, and our bodies washed with pure water. (Hebrews 10:20-22 KJV)

So, with hearts full of the adventure of faith, and with our Bibles open, let's dare to climb up to the porch of Heaven, and see the four great pillars upon which the entrance to our Rest is founded!

1) *There will be the amazing and glorious return of our Lord Jesus Christ.* Jesus did not leave us without a promise to return. The Bridegroom has not divorced His Bride. For our sake Jesus came, suffered, died, ascended, and will return. Think about this: Did Jesus purchase us at so great a price – His own blood – only to then forget about us and leave us to weep and sin, groan and die, without coming to rescue us again?

43

No! Jesus has *promised* His return, and left us many pledges of it:

And if I go and prepare a place for you, I will come back and take you to be with me that you also may be where I am. (John 14:3)

Now learn this lesson from the fig tree: As soon as its twigs get tender and its leaves come out, you know that summer is near. Even so, when you see all these things, you know that He is near, right at the door. (Matthew 24:32,33)

In fact, the very evils we see multiplying all around us: nations at war, brothers hating each other, believers being increasingly persecuted, Jerusalem's turmoil, are, says Jesus, sure signs of history closing and our Bridegroom returning:

At that time they will see the Son of Man coming in a cloud with power and great glory. When these things begin to take place, stand up and lift up your heads, because your redemption is drawing near. (Luke 21:27,28)

Christian! What is our great hope if it is not the return of Him who loves us? Do not be afraid! It *cannot* be that He will not come for us. His love for us is not lukewarm as ours so often is for Him. He *must* come for us. The King who once humbled Himself to suffer will return in triumph. He will take full possession of His purchased prize. Jesus has asked us to forsake all for *Him*. Will He then forget and forsake *us*? May our hearts not entertain, even for a moment, the thought that Jesus will forsake His Bride.

He told us plainly that it was better for us if He, for a season, left us. "But very truly I tell you, it is for your good that I am going away. Unless I go away, the Advocate [Holy Spirit] will not come to you; but if I go, I will send him to you." (John 16:7)

We have to trust Him for this. *He* knows that it was best to leave us for a season, and send His Holy Spirit to us. *He* knows that He has accomplished His work of redemption. *He* knows that it is better for us that He intercede for us than to be bodily present with us. *He* knows that He had to go and prepare a place for us. *He* knows our time here is short and that we will soon be with Him. *He* knows that there are precious others ... countless redeemed souls ... now in Heaven rejoicing with Him. *He* knows that it is better for us to walk now by faith than by sight. And *we* need to rest in what *He* knows.

What a day it will be when our faith is replaced by sight! Imprisoned here in this valley of tears, we will be liberated by our Lord Himself. And, if His first coming, lowly and humble as it was, still commanded the singing of angels to shepherds and a star to guide men from distant lands to worship a baby in the poverty of an animal shed, imagine how His return – not in poverty but in glory – will command the very ends of the earth to acknowledge Him as King of kings? "Every eye will see Him" (Revelation 1:7) as with shouts of victory and peace and with blessings He will come for His Bride!

The return of Jesus is to be a continual source of strength and endurance for us who await Him. Time and time again the Apostles in their letters encourage and remind us of His coming for us. This being true, why do we so often forget His promised appearing and seek comfort elsewhere? Imagine an embattled city awaiting rescue. They have no comfort besides the promised coming of their king. We can see the residents searching eagerly and waiting expectantly for their faithful deliverer to come. Scarcely does a moment go by without their desired rescue being on their minds and on their lips. Their future hope gives them present joy. And, when they hear the battle cry of their approaching king, how a shout of victory begins to sound from them!

Just pause and dwell on the day when the King of kings, the Lion of Judah, breaks the sky with His appearing. Consider the day of the Church's deliverance! Think about the shock of the careless when they see Him whom they shrugged off and of the mockers when they hear the voice of Him whom they hated. Both the saints and the sinners will be transfixed and transformed at His coming.

Believer! Shouldn't we be crying out in prayer every day saying: "Lord Jesus, let your Kingdom come!"? Should not the bride call out to the Bridegroom, "Come!"? Little wonder the Bible closes with the expectant prayer:

He who testifies to these things says, "Yes, I am coming soon."
Amen. Come, Lord Jesus.
(Revelation 22:20)

2) *We will see the wonderful raising of our bodies in glory to be reunited with our souls.* Call it the second pillar of the porch or the second stream that leads to the Paradise of God, whichever image helps you to see and rejoice in this truth. In the resurrection of our bodies we see on display the infinite power of the love of God!

Do you think I am gullible to believe this? Will you listen to me as I plead the case for God? Look at the very world we inhabit. Who suspends it and holds it in space? Look at the vast oceans of water. Who keeps them in their boundaries? Who directs the moon to keep the oceans' tides? Look at the Sun, it is a million times bigger than the earth. Yet it is held in its place as it travels its course and burns on and on without fail. How? Think with me! If God can perform these great wonders, can He not resurrect *your* body?

We see all around us, every day, God's phenomenal works. But we grow so used to them that we have ceased to wonder at them. Yet they should encourage us toward trusting in the resurrection of our bodies. Is it harder for God to resurrect your body than to create and sustain a universe? We need to take our eyes off the bones and the dust and put them on the promises and power of God! Just as surely as we lie down at night only to awake in the morning, so shall our bodies lie down in death only to awake in glory. Don't fear losing your body ... you will be getting a better one! Don't fear losing this "tent" because an eternal building, sure and strong, not made by human hands, but by God Himself, is waiting for you.

For we know that if the earthly tent we live in is destroyed, we have a building from God, an eternal house in heaven, not built by human hands. Meanwhile we groan, longing to be clothed instead with our heavenly dwelling, because when we are clothed, we will not be found naked. For while we are in this tent, we groan and are burdened, because we do not wish to be unclothed but to be clothed instead with our heavenly dwelling, so that what is mortal may be swallowed up by life. Now the one who has fashioned us for this very purpose is God, who has given us the Spirit as a deposit, guaranteeing what is to come. (2 Corinthians 5:1-5)

The Bible tells us that as a seed is sown perishable, so we will be, but only to be raised imperishable. As we are sown in dust and dishonour, we will be raised in honour and glory. Our bodies are now earthly, but they will then be spiritual (1 Corinthians 15:35-54).

Believer! Believe this! Live in victory *now* through God's *promise*, knowing that one day you will live in victory through God's *performance*. As the grave could not hold Jesus, so it will not hold those who are in Jesus: "For if we believe that Jesus died and rose again, even so them also which sleep in Jesus will God bring with him." (1 Thessalonians 4:14; 16-17 KJV). Write on your heart Jesus' words of victory: "Because I live, you also will live." (John 14:19) We have more than just this life! Our lives are "hidden with Christ in God." (Colossians 3:3) Unbelief sees only the grave. Faith sees beyond the grave to eternity.

The Bible tells us to rejoice in this knowledge. So, go on and gladden your hearts and rest now in the sure hope of your future Rest.

For the Lord himself will come down from heaven, with a loud command, with the voice of the archangel and with the trumpet call of God, and the dead in Christ will rise first. After that, we who are still alive and are left will be caught up together with them in the clouds to meet the Lord in the air. And so we will be with the Lord for ever. Therefore encourage one another with these words. (1 Thessalonians 4:16-18)

3) The third pillar of the entrance to our Rest is the *public and awesome day in which we all appear before the Judgment Seat of Christ.* On that great and solemn day every believer in Jesus will have declared publically the verdict they have received now by faith: "Justified and Acquitted by the merits of Jesus!"

And then, Jesus will judge the world.

On that day the kindness *and* the severity of God will be evident for all to see. All of history will be summoned before Jesus. No one can avoid that Great Day! Young and old, rich and poor, every nation and tribe will then meet the Holy God they scorned and mocked, or simply carelessly and foolishly disregarded. But what a day of joy for the redeemed! The many who have waited and looked for this day shall embrace their hearts' desire.

I know I am writing this book to refresh the saints, not to warn the unbeliever. But perhaps you are rejecting Jesus and His Gospel and these few lines have fallen into your hands. Now are the days when Christ will, but you won't. But the day will come when you will, but Christ won't. It will be too late. I plead with you, with all my heart and nerve, and beg you - get alone with God and take time with Him and your soul. I promise you it will be the most valuable little bit of time you have ever spent, for it will affect your eternity. I do charge you, in the Name of the Lord Jesus Christ, to not take this lightly, but – right now – to do your business with God and surrender to Christ the King while you still have a chance. Ask you own heart: "Should I waste another day when I have already wasted so many?" "Is it true? Will *I* appear before Jesus?" "What should I do? Am I not already overdue in my need to deal with God?"

Today you will find a welcoming God. But not someday.

But while they were on their way to buy the oil, the bridegroom arrived. The virgins who were ready went in with him to the wedding banquet. And the door was shut.
Later the others also came. "Lord, Lord," they said, "open the door for us!"
But he replied, "Truly I tell you, I don't know you."
(Matthew 25:10-12)

'Today, if you hear his voice, do not harden your hearts
as you did in the rebellion.'
(Hebrews 3:15)

But, dear Christian, while we look upon that day with reverence and awe, we do not look upon it with a craven fear. It is the great day of our vindication before God and the watching world. It is the day when what we have received now by faith – justification – will be proclaimed for all to hear. And, this same Jesus, who is the Great Judge, is the Jesus who came not to condemn the world but to save it, and who promised His Father that He would lose none of all that He had given to Him. The Judge loves us! The Judge has made atonement for our sins by His own blood! Will he then undo what He has already done? Having redeemed us at infinite cost, will He then give us back to the Hell from which He purchased us? For the unbeliever that day is one to dread, to try to forget, to joke or wish away. But to the believer, the anticipation of that day, when Jesus' saving power is displayed beyond all doubt, should bring a sweetness here and now.

Since we have now been justified by his blood, how much more shall we be saved from God's wrath through him! For if, while we were God's enemies, we were reconciled to him through the death of his Son, how much more, having been reconciled, shall we be saved through his life! Not only is this so, but we also boast in God through our Lord Jesus Christ, through whom we have now received reconciliation. (Romans 5:9-11)

But, there is even more, almost too much to believe. Far from just not being condemned in the Judgment, we will actually judge *with* Jesus. There, the Great King and Judge of all people and angels will bring *us* into His firm and we will, somehow, sit with Him and agree with Him in that Great Day.

Or do you not know that the Lord's people will judge the world? ... Do you not know that we will judge angels? (1 Corinthians 6:2,3)

If the Bible itself did not say such a thing, it would be the greatest arrogance and presumption for us to ever even imagine it. But may it instead serve to humble us and make us marvel at the goodness of God: Sinners, deserving judgment, saved by grace, joining Jesus in the work of the final judgment!

Take joy in this, dear believer! Get on and live fearlessly and valiantly, for your Saviour and Lord has your destiny securely held for you.

4) *Next, we will experience our Coronation, Enthronement, and Receiving of the Kingdom which Jesus Christ shares with us.* As Jesus Christ is King of kings, enthroned forever, so we, through our union with Him, shall be enthroned with and under Him to serve as kings and priests forever.

The Bible teaches that all who "long for His appearing" will - from *Him,* not from an angel, nor archangel, nor Moses or Elijah, nor Peter - but *from Jesus Himself,* receive a "crown of righteousness" (2 Timothy 4:6-8). And it seems that the Word of God teaches that according to the degree of faithfulness exercised in this life, we shall be rewarded in eternity with meaningful (not empty) employment as co-rulers with Jesus (1 Corinthians 3:10-14; Luke 19:11-27). Since Eden, God's design has been that we would rule as His viceroys over creation (Genesis 1:26). He has not forgotten that design, but has redeemed us that we might fulfill His original purpose for us.

With a solemn authority He shall enthrone us:

And he shall set the sheep on his right hand, but the goats on the left. Then shall the King say unto them on his right hand, Come, ye blessed of my Father, inherit the kingdom prepared for you from the foundation of the world ... (Matthew 25: 33-35 KJV)

Consider the joy in that proclamation: Here the King of the Universe is holding out His scepter to us, we who have been redeemed by His blood, and inviting us to Him! In the Kingdom that is to come we each will have the whole of Jesus, and none will lack any fullness in Him, even as each beam of light has the whole of the sun, and no beam of light lacks any of the sun. The eternal love of God has prepared and founded this Kingdom for us, and us for it. For this He has purposed us: That we, who have received unimagined love, might rule with Him in a Kingdom of love.

But, I see a problem here! If we are justified by grace through faith *alone*, how does that fit in with talk of heavenly rewards that are in any way based upon our care for the poor, love towards others, consecration to spiritual things, etc.? Am I in some way promoting a "gospel" where we contribute our merit to salvation? I think we need to be very clear here: Justification, that is, the way in which God declares a sinner pardoned and righteous through the merits of Jesus, is based solely upon the grace of God which we receive by faith *alone*. We contribute nothing to it but *need*. We can do nothing to merit our justification before a holy God. Justification does not differ from one believer to another. It is an instantaneous, declarative act of God through the atonement of Jesus Christ. Clear?

But, *rewards* are different from justification! Rewards differ between believers. Some apply more diligence than others in living out their salvation. Some, as it were, build with gold, silver, and precious jewels, others with wood, hay, and stubble (1 Corinthians 3:10ff). The work of some will prove to be of eternal value. The work of others will be seen to be of only earthly value. We are not saved by works, but we are saved to work, and the capacity of our vessels to hold eternal joy, and the scope of our reign with Christ, will be determined not by justification, but by our growth in grace.

We have now explored the four streams which lead to our Rest. We are finding ourselves safe in Jesus' Heaven. Now, let us begin to explore the wonders and privileges that are ours in Heaven and ask if there is anything that even closely compares with what God has in store for us.

Scriptures to Ponder:

We know that the whole creation has been groaning as in the pains of childbirth right up to the present time. Not only so, but we ourselves, who have the firstfruits of the Spirit, groan inwardly as we wait eagerly for our adoption to sonship, the redemption of our bodies. For in this hope we were saved. But hope that is seen is no hope at all. Who hopes for what they already have? (Romans 8:22-24)

But our citizenship is in heaven. And we eagerly await a Saviour from there, the Lord Jesus Christ, who, by the power that enables him to bring everything under his control, will transform our lowly bodies so that they will be like his glorious body. (Philippians 3:20-21)

So we make it our goal to please him, whether we are at home in the body or away from it. For we must all appear before the judgment seat of Christ, so that each of us may receive what is due to us for the things done while in the body, whether good or bad. (1 Corinthians 5:9-10)

Questions to Consider:

1) How should the fact of the coming return of Jesus empower us and motivate us today? How can it be both a source of reverent fear and of great joy?

2) In what ways does the hope of the resurrection of your body in glory transform your view of life today? Are you shaped more by your past than by your future? Should you be?

Chapter Six

Reason Tells Us of the Wonders of Our Rest

We expect the Bible to extol the wonders of our Rest. In due time we will explore the Bible's Heaven. But first, I want to demonstrate that reason proves the wonders of Heaven. No, reason alone is not a sufficient authority for us, and yes, we do need to go beyond it and build our case on the revealed truth of God, but reason is not worthless. And, particularly where unbelievers are concerned (those who scoff at the Bible), reason can be an able help in our endeavour to help them see the wonders of God and the Gospel. Reason also helps the Heaven - and Hell - bound see that Heaven *must* be better than anything else.

So, let's apply the philosopher's argument in testing the worth of Heaven.

1) *The destination is always more treasured than the journey.* As pleasant or important as the journey might be, it goes without saying that the point of the journey is not the journey itself, but the destination. In a journey, all things – the food eaten, the route taken, the vehicles used – are just a means to the end. If any part of the journey is worthy of praise, it not because of itself, but because of what it contributes to reaching that which is worthy of *more* praise: the goal.

You will agree with me that the goal of our faith is our salvation from sin, unto Heaven, for the glory of God. We do not pray, preach, baptize, receive bread and wine, or even believe, for their own sake, but for the greater purpose of entering our Rest. All these things are just ways to Jesus - who is our Rest. Jesus is the way and the destination. Is it not

55

abundantly clear that Jesus and Jesus' Heaven is the desired destination for the Christian, and therefore to be more treasured than all else?

The kingdom of heaven is like treasure hidden in a field. When a man found it, he hid it again, and then in his joy went and sold all he had and bought that field. (Matthew 13:44)

2) *It is reasonable that the last will be the best.* As this is our usual experience in the things of *this* life, it makes sense to assume that this will be the experience of the saints' *eternal* life. Consider a feast - all things build to the main course. Planting moves toward a harvest. In a concert all things, even the moments of disharmony, move to a great climax. In a play all scenes, even those with tension and tragedy, build to a high point. In a tournament, all events shall lead to the final, championship game.

Certainly, what we see in daily life is like a seed compared to the full flower. In our journey with Jesus, we are beginning with small things, but we are traveling toward great things. If the end is wonderful, then the journey, even if fraught with hardship, is wonderful as well. If we reap in joy, then the sowing in tears was worth it. If we know any goodness here, it must be just a foretaste of the ultimate goodness for which our hearts long.

For our light and momentary troubles are achieving for us an eternal glory that far outweighs them all.
(2 Corinthians 4:17)

3) *The greater the value of something, the more tragic its loss.* What loss can be greater than the loss of our Rest? Every other loss can either be mended or done without. Money, health,

reputation, possessions, can be recovered or lived without. Even your physical life can be lost. But, how can you live without the hope of Heaven? No wonder Jesus Himself tells us that the losing of Heaven leaves us with "weeping and gnashing of teeth" (Matthew 8:12). When things most valued are lost forever, those who have lived foolishly will then see their true value. We can live without almost anything, for all things beneath God are of comparatively little value. But how can we live without God and His Heaven?

Then I beg you, father, send Lazarus to my family, for I have five brothers. Let him warn them, so that they will not also come to this place of torment. (Luke 16:27,28)

4) *That which can neither be given nor taken by man is better than that which can.* Jesus has the key to true treasure: Heaven. He will not misplace His key! He is the One who blesses believers with grace for this life, eternal life, and eternal rewards. Without question, every good thing along the way, every grace for this journey, every deliverance from trouble, every mercy in the midst of trouble, bears the stamp and trademark of our Good and Gracious Father. All these lead us to our God-given Rest.

What God gives, no person can take away. The gifts of God, culminating in Heaven itself, are unassailable. A persecutor might take your freedom or even your life, but he cannot take Heaven from you. Men can lock us in a prison, but no man can lock us out of Heaven. A man can throw you out of his kingdom, but he cannot cast you from God's.

Think about simpler things: Can a man blow out the sun? Can he stop the planets in their course? Even easier, can he stop the dew from settling or command the clouds to hold their rain? Can he with a word stop a river or halt the tides? These all are small things compared to overcoming the salvation and promises of God! It would be easier to throw away the moon than to throw a believer out of Jesus' Heaven! No person can dam the rivers of His love, halt the dew of His grace, rebuke the influence of His Spirit, or darken the light of His smile. If He allows, a tyrant can kill our bodies, but no mere man ... even if the whole world fears him ... can touch our souls. It is not even in the believer's own power to undo the saving, keeping grace of God in his life.

There is no place like Heaven, and no place of safety like the believers' Rest, because no person can give it, and no person can take it.

My sheep listen to my voice; I know them, and they follow me. I give them eternal life, and they shall never perish; no one will snatch them out of my hand. My Father, who has given them to me, is greater than all; no one can snatch them out of my Father's hand. I and the Father are one. (John 10:27-30)

> *As we have heard,*
> *so we have seen*
> *in the city of the Lord Almighty,*
> *in the city of our God:*
> *God makes her secure*
> *for ever.*
> (Psalm 48:8)

5) *Whatever makes you better is better, so whatever makes you your best, is the best.* What can make us our best but Heaven? Money does not make us better – in fact, it ruins many of us. Grace makes us better, but Glory brings out the best in us.

Something is good if it does us good. But unless in doing us good it actually *makes* us good, it is really of no use to us. Rarely will earthly wealth (seen by many as "good") actually *make* us good. We need something inside, changing our hearts from bad to good if it is to be of benefit. If, even in this life, our hearts are with Jesus in Heaven, then *even now* we are being changed into the people God designs us to be. But it is hard to have hearts in Heaven while our bodies are prospering on earth. Sadly, seldom do body and soul prosper together! Whatever humbles the body so that the soul can prosper in Jesus is a blessing! And, when death finally sets us free from these shrines of sin, so that we are with Jesus, then and there we will be at our best!

A true Christian cares more for his soul than his body, and weeps more for his unseen sin than he delights in his visible strength. His hope is in Heaven, for there he knows he will be at his best ... finally!

> *Yet I am always with you;*
> *you hold me by my right hand.*
> *You guide me with your counsel,*
> *and afterwards you will take me into glory.*
> *Whom have I in heaven but you?*
> *And earth has nothing I desire besides you.*
> *My flesh and my heart may fail,*
> *but God is the strength of my heart*
> *and my portion for ever.*
> (Psalm 73:23-36)

6) *The cost at which something is gained proves its worth.* Heaven cost something more precious than anything else in all the universe. Therefore, it must be more precious than anything else.

Have you ever stopped and really *thought* about what Jesus paid to purchase Rest for you? If Heaven was purchased at such a price for you (and you for Heaven), how can you discount your soul, allowing it to be bought by and for lesser things?

Think about the cost to the Holy Spirit: grieved, resisted, and ignored, yet He loved and wooed on and on. Think about the cost to pastors and ministers and friends who pled and prayed for you, wept and lost sleep for you, refusing to give up. Think of what it cost you! Friendships? Wealth? Popularity? Health?

What can be as valuable as Jesus and His Heaven? It is easier to destroy than to build. It is easier to ruin your soul than to save it. It is always easier to coast than to climb, to descend than ascend. Jesus, who is the Way, and knows the way, tells us that it is narrow, perilous, and costly. Those who have walked it well tell us that the way is strewn with tribulations, but that the journey is worth the strife, because of the value of the destination.

For you know that it was not with perishable things such as silver or gold that you were redeemed from the empty way of life handed down to you from your ancestors, but with the precious blood of Christ, a lamb without blemish or defect. (1 Peter 1:18,19)

7) *The better the blessings something gives, the more valuable it is.* Since Heaven brings the most abundant blessing, it is therefore of more worth than all else. Nothing blesses like the Gospel – super, abundant, useful, meaningful blessings. God does more than just supply our basic needs in saving us, He provides an abundance of goodness.

60

But in this life, even with all the blessings God gives now, He in His wisdom saves the fullness for later. He leaves us – at least to some degree – hungry here. Hunger leads to seeking and dependence. Hunger forces us to look to Jesus, and to His Heaven. If we were 'full' here, we would not hunger for being with Jesus in Heaven. Every blessing we receive here is just a foretaste of what is to come in superabundance in Glory.

So, we praise God for both the foretaste now and the feast to come! For it is when we enter our Rest that we finally thirst and hunger no more. There, the super-abundance of blessing will bring forth from us a superabundance of praise … such as we have never experienced in this life!

Then I heard every creature in heaven and on earth and under the earth and on the sea, and all that is in them, saying:

> *'To him who sits on the throne and to the Lamb*
> *be praise and honour and glory and power,*
> *for ever and ever!'*
> *… Never again will they hunger;*
> *never again will they thirst.*
> (Revelation 5:13; 7:16)

8) *It makes sense that if the wisest and best among us time and again conclude that something is the best, then it probably is.* Of course, the best and wisest people are not God, but frail disciples. Nevertheless, we find consistent testimony to their pursuit of Heaven as their goal, and being with Jesus forever as their top priority. When we look at the lives of the holiest and happiest people, we, without fail, see them hungering for what their natural eyes cannot see, but what their eyes of faith are beginning to see. Most of them will tell us that they tried to find happiness in the fleeting things of this world, but their

hearts were again and again left vacant. They will tell us that their hearts are now set on Heaven. They will tell us that they have discovered, often with bitter tears, the emptiness of the best this life has to offer. They will earnestly plead with us to make Jesus and His Heaven our goal, and to rest our souls only in His Rest.

They can say with the Psalmist:

> *Better is one day in your courts*
> *than a thousand elsewhere;*
> *I would rather be a doorkeeper in the house of my God*
> *than dwell in the tents of the wicked.*
> (Psalm 84:10)

9) Finally, *if something contains and sustains all other truly good things, then it must be the very best of all.* Every truly good thing springs from God and empties itself back into God. He is the source and the goal of every river of blessing. He is the spring and the ocean of all that is good.

There was a time – before creation - when all goodness was within God, the Father, the Son, and the Holy Spirit. And now, every good thing we know in this created life is contingent and dependent upon Him who is Good and who pours out rivers of life and goodness. But, these rivers also flow into Him, even as raindrops come from the ocean, to the rivers, and back to the ocean. So, will you, when you are in the very presence of God, be lacking any truly good thing? Will we, who have been quenching our thirst from the river of blessing, find lack in the ocean of blessing? We have been walking by the light of a lamp. Will we be disappointed when we walk in the full day of the sun? We have found some goodness in God's creatures. Will we be disappointed when we are in the presence of their Creator?

Do not be afraid that you will somehow find that God's Heaven is missing some good thing you need. God contains all goodness, and Heaven – God's home - must therefore be without equal. God will not deceive you! Your Rest will be *better* than expected! Every trial, every tear, every penny invested in His Kingdom now will be outweighed by joy and happiness and true treasure in our Rest. Give yourself with abandon to our Good God and He will return you to yourself better than before!

Do not be afraid, little flock, for your Father has been pleased to give you the kingdom. Sell your possessions and give to the poor. Provide purses for yourselves that will not wear out, a treasure in heaven that will never fail, where no thief comes near and no moth destroys. For where your treasure is, there your heart will be also. (Luke 12:32-34)

Scriptures to Rejoice in:

Praise be to the God and Father of our Lord Jesus Christ! In his great mercy he has given us new birth into a living hope through the resurrection of Jesus Christ from the dead, and into an inheritance that can never perish, spoil or fade. This inheritance is kept in heaven for you, who through faith are shielded by God's power until the coming of the salvation that is ready to be revealed in the last time. (1 Peter 1:3-5)

I want to know Christ – yes, to know the power of his resurrection and participation in his sufferings, becoming like him in his death, and so, somehow, attaining to the resurrection from the dead. Not that I have already obtained all this, or have already arrived at my goal, but I press on to take hold of that for which Christ Jesus took hold of me. Brothers and sisters, I do not consider myself yet to have taken hold of it. But one thing I do:

63

forgetting what is behind and straining towards what is ahead, I press on towards the goal to win the prize for which God has called me heavenwards in Christ Jesus. (Philippians 3:10-14)

Questions to Consider:

1) Consider the cost to God of your salvation. How does this shape your perspective upon your life and your priorities?

2) Considering the value of Heaven, are you ordering your life in a way that reflects your hope of entering your Rest?

3) What does the fact of Heaven say about the character and nature of God?

4) Is your life shaped more by disappointments or victories from your past, or by your hope for the future – Heaven?

Chapter Seven

The Wonders of Our Rest

Reason has shown us some wonders. But the Bible will show us more. We have stood on the porch, we have pulled back the curtain just a little. Now it is time to go farther! Like Moses before the bush, let's remove from our feet the shoes of irreverence and human wisdom, for we are standing on holy ground.

1) Our Rest is a *purchased Rest.* Heaven is the fruit of the suffering of Jesus Christ. His blood bought our Rest. Whatever other blessings Jesus has secured for us, the greatest blessing is Heaven. And this purchase is not solely for our benefit, but Jesus also is receiving the reward for His bleeding and dying:

'Here am I, and the children God has given me.'
(Hebrews 2:13)

Jesus Christ ... gave himself for us to redeem us from all wickedness and to purify for himself a people that are his very own, eager to do what is good.
(Titus 2:14)

In God's garden of love, every flower that grows is a precious expression of His love for us. But it is the blood-red flower that displays His love the most. What a joy it is to rest in the very heart of God knowing that it is a heart of love – love proven on a cross - which purchased sinners from sin to Himself. Even now, before Heaven, we can and must have the love of God ever before the eyes of our souls. There is *no greater love* than the dying, redeeming, purchasing, love of God through Jesus Christ.

Jesus died to save us from the deserved wrath of God. I do not need to fully understand the depths of God's saving ways in order to receive, rejoice in, and declare the wonders of the Gospel. I do not need to enter endless speculations about particulars - most of which I cannot understand and do not need to understand.

> *My mouth will tell of your righteous deeds,*
> *of your saving acts all day long –*
> *though I know not how to relate them all.*
> (Psalm 71:15)

Beginning now, but reaching fullness in eternity, it is and will be the great joy of the Redeemed to behold both the Purchaser and the price paid. Today, His heart is wide open to us, while ours is just ajar to Him, but then ... Oh! ...our hearts will be wide open to His as His is to us. We will be clothed in the righteous robes which He has provided, robes paid for by His own precious blood.

And they sang a new song, saying: 'You are worthy to take the scroll and to open its seals, because you were slain, and with your blood you purchased for God persons from every tribe and language and people and nation. (Revelation 5:9)

2) Our Rest is a *Free Rest,* purchased and free. Costly to Jesus, free to us. What did the Lord ever see in me that He should clothe me in such a costly salvation – at *His* expense? "Lord! Holy Spirit! Cause me to marvel at the costly freeness of my salvation!" Poor, filthy, sinful, crippled, enemies of God, and yet Jesus purchases us from sin and Satan and gives us Himself and Heaven. May we never grow used to this. May it always surprise and amaze us that we receive Heaven as a *gift!*

If Rest were only obtained by our worthiness, we, like John the Apostle, would have cause to weep: "Who is worthy ... no one on earth!" (Revelation 5:4ff) But Jesus the "Lion of the tribe of Judah, the Root of David – *He* is worthy," and it is in Him that we are counted as worthy.

We need to be gripped by the wonder of this: Jesus has redeemed us for Himself at great cost to *Himself*, that we might receive Him to ourselves at no cost to *ourselves*. A pope or priest might pretend to sell you salvation. They might ask for your money, but Jesus never will. Religions the world over are founded upon the – impossible - idea that we can somehow earn our way to God. People pay, strive, labour, sweat, and bleed, foolishly thinking that they can somehow merit what the Bible says can only be received freely by faith. The Kingdom is for the poor in purse and in spirit.

(By the way... let me say while I can ... the Gospel is free, and it is therefore abhorrent when pretending ministers of the Gospel try to profit from it. Of course, a labourer is worthy of his hire, but watch your motive! The Apostle Paul could honestly say that he had not coveted anyone's silver or gold or clothing (Acts 20:33). A true servant of Christ would rather offer the Gospel for free to all than do anything to hinder the work of the Gospel by seeking to profit from what is offered freely by God. "Unlike so many, we do not peddle the word of God for profit. On the contrary, in Christ we speak before God with sincerity, as those sent from God." (2 Corinthians 2:17))

Back to Heaven! The gate of Heaven swings on these two hinges: *Purchased* and *Free.* We paid nothing for God the Father's love, nothing for His Son's love, or for the love of the Holy Spirit. We did not have to buy our grace or God's pardon. Even our faith is a gift! So, we will not buy Heaven either. Our Rest is free! What a relief to the broken-hearted! What a fountain in the desert of sin! The distance between what we deserve in ourselves and what we receive in Jesus is as wide as the ocean. God has ordered our salvation such that there is no room for human merit or boasting, but that our joy might be full and His grace might be magnified.

If the gate of Hell is signed "Deserved," then the door to Life is signed "The Free Gift of God."

The Spirit and the bride say, "Come!" And let the one who hears say, "Come!" Let the one who is thirsty come; and let the one who wishes take the free gift of the water of life. (Revelation 22:17)

3) God's Rest is the purchased, free gift prepared *for His People alone.* God could have decided that Heaven would be for *all,* that none would be outside of His saving mercy. Or, He could have decided that *none* should be saved, but all go to a deserved wrath. Or, He could have decided that *one* should be rescued as a sure sign of His mercy. But in His wisdom God has not decided to save all, or none, or one, but *many* … in fact a number so great that no one can number it except God Himself (Revelation 7:9).

Now, none of us dare to demand that God explain Himself here. Nor do we try to explain the secrets of God's wisdom and ways. But, having said that, may I tremble and venture to propose a reason why God has not saved all, or none, or one, but many?

If you are a saved sinner, if you have found your name written in God's Book of Life, if you have come to Jesus in response to His gracious call to you, then do you not fear and worship and revere God *even more* because He had mercy *on you*? You *know* you are undeserving. You *know* there is no good in you to distinguish you from your unbelieving neighbor. You *know* that you are no better than the next person. Yet! God has had mercy on *you*! Doesn't this particular mercy cause you to marvel and worship? And then, when shared with a company of others who have received this same mercy, is not this marvel and worship multiplied many times? So perhaps God, in designing to not have mercy on all, nor on none, nor on one, He is producing the greatest gratitude, marvel, and wonder in the great company of those He has purchased from every tribe and tongue and nation ... all to His greater glory and our greater happiness.

I should leave my adventure there. Better to put our hands over our mouths and worship:

Oh, the depth of the riches of the wisdom and knowledge of God!
How unsearchable his judgments,
and his paths beyond tracing out!
"Who has known the mind of the Lord?
Or who has been his counselor?"
"Who has ever given to God,
that God should repay them?"
For from him and through him and for him are all things.
To him be the glory forever! Amen.
(Romans 11:33-36)

Today the world scoffs and mocks at your pursuit of holiness and your refusal to enter into some of its practices. Be assured that one day all will be understood, and without any explanation from you. In that day you and I will see – even more clearly than we do now – that our battle for holiness of heart and life was the only fitting response to our having been made God's precious possession.

But you are a chosen people, a royal priesthood, a holy nation,
God's special possession, that you may declare the praises of him

who called you out of darkness into his wonderful light. (1 Peter 2:9)

4) Next, our Rest is *a precious fellowship of all the Redeemed and the angels of God.* Jesus' Heaven is not some drifting off into "nothingness," or disappearing like a drop into the vast ocean. It is a glorious, conscious gathering of all the redeemed! Imagine, all believers finally *perfect* - with Jesus Himself in our midst. You might want to imagine it as a symphony, where all the players draw their tune from one source, the conductor, and in so doing join in one great harmonious anthem of praise – with the angels themselves adding their beauty.

Here our symphony weeps and fasts and waits together. We play often in a minor key. The theme is often tragic. There are even moments of dissonance. But then! No tragedy, no minor key, but fullness of joy and perfection of praise! We can be certain of this: As we have been together in the battle, the tears, the labour, the hardship (and even still our fellowship has been sweet), so shall we be together in the victory, the reward, the deliverance. We have been together in being despised and scorned, so shall we together receive our crown of righteousness from our wonderful Jesus. Our brothers, who have been imprisoned while we have prayed for them, will be with us in freedom while we rejoice with them. Delivered from prison to palace! We have gone through the nights of sadness together, so we will live in the day of gladness together.

Of course, the great joy of Heaven will be our fellowship with Jesus. And we dare not anticipate being with those whom we love here more than we anticipate being with Jesus. (Sadly, Christians often talk more about being with their friends and loved ones in Heaven than with Jesus.) But, if Jesus has commanded us to love one another *here*, and if it is part of His joy to see us now walking in fellowship, how much more will

He rejoice in us loving each other perfectly in His wonderful presence! "Here am I, and the children God has given me." (Hebrews 2:13)

If following Jesus with our brothers and sisters has been sweet here, what sweetness will we enjoy together in Heaven? What a day of rejoicing for us (and for Jesus!) when we are with those with whom we have here prayed and battled and suffered! Imagine being with those with whom we have here failed to love well and perhaps broken fellowship ... what a day! If today, right now, we can love our brothers and sisters in the light of that day, looking into their redeemed, but still flawed faces in anticipation of the glory that awaits them, how our fellowship *right now* will be transformed!

It is often asked: "Will we know one another in Heaven?" and, if so, in what manner? Listen: What we know now, with the exception of sin, will not be diminished, but enhanced. We know this is true with regard to our knowledge of the Lord. We can trust it will be true with regard to our knowledge of His people as well. Perhaps we can liken our future knowledge of one another to the light of a candle when the sun rises. The candle gave its light while in the dark, but now that light has been overwhelmed by a greater light. So, we will certainly no longer know each other by the dimness of our current knowledge: earthly fame, status, reputation, wealth, passing physical attributes such as beauty or disfigurement, gender, or any other outward knowledge. No, we will then know each other somehow in and through Jesus Christ. Trivial knowledge will be replaced by genuine knowledge. Earthly titles, temporal honours, will be replaced by knowing one another as we really are, in our relation to Jesus. No more misunderstanding one another, no more shallow, surface measuring of each other.

71

Depth, meaning, truth shall replace what we have come to see as normal here.

Think of the saints of old, men and women that we have read about and heard of, but never met! What about brothers and sisters around the world that we have prayed and wept for but only imagined? How sweet will be our unhindered knowledge of them in the full light of Jesus! That gathering will be more joyful than any we have had here in this life. Imagine: If our fellowship below ... in this current dimness ... is often so precious and dear, what will it be like in the full light of Heaven? Here we have the sweetness of holiness *and* the bitterness of sin. There, nothing will embitter and sour the company. And, if you are grieved now in being misunderstood, undervalued, brushed aside, overlooked, there is a day ahead when you will be loved, valued, known, and embraced as you longed for here.

Indeed, in our Rest we shall - in fullness - be "no longer foreigners and strangers, but fellow citizens with God's people and also members of his household ..." (Ephesians 2:19)

Dear friends, now we are children of God, and what we will be has not yet been made known. But we know that when Christ appears, we shall be like him, for we shall see him as he is. (1 John 3:2)

But you have come ... to the city of the living God, the heavenly Jerusalem ... to thousands upon thousands of angels in joyful assembly ... to the spirits of the righteous made perfect, to Jesus the mediator of a new covenant, and to the sprinkled blood that speaks a better word than the blood of Abel. (Hebrews 12:22-24)
5) In our Rest our *Joy will come without hindrance directly from God.* Here there is so much interference! Our vision of God is so

cloudy. But the day is coming when we shall see our wonderful God face to face. We will be in His presence, and there we will draw our life and our joy directly from Him.

In this life, we do not know the *immediate* presence of God. We walk by faith, not by sight. All of our knowledge of God here and now is *mediated* through something. We know the Lord through His Word, with His people, by His Spirit, in His sacraments. These things are good and true and give us now a genuine knowledge of God. But as a stream flowing farther away from its pure source is muddied, so the good things that mediate God and His Gospel to us are muddied in their travels to us. Even though Jesus is the perfect pearl, He is often ministered to us via dirtied and diseased hands.

Even the best of us mar the wonders of God and His Gospel to one degree or another. The best we can share with one another now is but the half of what God has for us. The most amazing worship service you have experienced, the most stirring sermon you have ever heard, the best prayer time you have ever experienced ... the stain of our sin is found in each. Even an angel, if permitted to declare the marvels of God to us, would leave it deficient and defiled in some way.

But! The day is coming when the wonders of God will be made known to us without any hindrance. There will be no sun, for His face will be our sun. There will be communion, but no sacraments; rest, but no sleep; learning, but no written law. Jesus will share the new wine of the Kingdom with us, and we will all drink from the river of God's delights in our Father's house.

And I heard a loud voice from the throne saying, "Look! God's dwelling place is now among the people, and he will dwell with

them. They will be his people, and God himself will be with them and be their God." ... They will see his face, and his name will be on their foreheads. There will be no more night. They will not need the light of a lamp or the light of the sun, for the Lord God will give them light. And they will reign for ever and ever.
Revelation 21:3; 22:4,5)

6) Our Rest will be a *Welcome Rest.* Why do we fret so much over our arrival there? Why do we resist going to our Rest? We will find ourselves at our Rest not *one minute* too soon. God does everything in His perfect time. His works are never out of season. All His works of grace are timed exactly right ... even His common grace to His enemies. Sun, rain, harvest, day, night, winter, and summer, all of God's doings are welcome expressions of His graciousness towards us – and always on time.

How much more so will Heaven be His fullest, perfect, most timely grace to us! What a welcome joy will be Jesus' Heaven! After a long night of sorrow, how welcome is the morning? After a seemingly endless winter how welcome is the thaw of spring? When a sailor has for many days sailed through stormy seas and starless nights, how welcome is that safe and peaceful harbour? When we have become weary of sin and trials, and sickness and death, and mourning and pain, how welcome will be our Rest!

Think of all the dangers to our souls during this pilgrimage. This life is a *war.* The enemy never sleeps. Our watching and warring have been ceaseless. Oh, to enter the welcome peace that our Rest assures! Our going from this earth to Heaven will be more welcome than if we were transported from a battlefield to a peaceful pasture, from a prison to a throne.
Why do we want to delay our Rest as long as we possibly can?

Do we love this present world too much?

Some of you know what it is like to wake in the morning wishing for night and to lie down at night hoping for the morning. These bodies! They can bring us great joy; they can be so useful, but - then – they can be racked by endless pain and paralyzing weakness. We are weary of sitting, weary of standing, weary of coming, weary of going, weary of lying down, weary of rising up, weary of people, weary of loneliness, weary of our own selves. We suffer war, taxes, bad news, fears, dangers, the ache of poverty, the boredom of riches ...

Give me that welcome Rest!

Think of your life as a Christian. For all the blessings you now enjoy, you still have to endure the pain of persecution, the sorrow of misunderstanding, the puzzle of unanswered prayer, the dangers of living in a rebel land, the sorrow of a cold heart, the frustration of relentless temptation, the anguish of rebellious loved ones, the bitter tears, dying friends, the terror of your fears, the haunting doubts, the shame of your sins, the dullness of your spirit, the pain of fractured relationships ...

Oh, for our welcome Rest!

I know, and you know as well, that sometimes when dear Christians are taken from us to their Rest, it is hard to believe that God has timed things right. How we needed them! "God! *Them?*" Yet we need even in such times to trust that God is good to *us* in bringing *them* to their welcome Rest. Believe me, your time will soon come, and we will then all be together in our Father's House, a place prepared for us by none other than Jesus Christ.

We are not more merciful than He. We are not wiser than He. We do not do better than He. God has proven Himself faithful to His people forever, and He will not fail us now. His Rest is always on time, in season, and welcome.

Therefore, my brothers and sisters, make every effort to confirm your calling and election. For if you do these things, you will never stumble, and you will receive a rich welcome into the eternal kingdom of our Lord and Saviour Jesus Christ. (2 Peter 1:10-12)

He has made everything beautiful in its time. He has also set eternity in the human heart ... (Ecclesiastes 3:11)

7) Our Rest will be a *Perfectly Suited* Rest. It will suit our true nature as living souls created in God's Image. It will suit our new natures as redeemed, perfected, spiritual beings. Fresh air and sunshine are good – unless you are a fish. Heaven will not suit you if you would rather have sinful pleasures and the passing things of this world. Heaven is made for Jesus Lovers, and Jesus Lovers are made for Heaven. It is for God and His redeemed ones. Our present bodies, weakened and corrupted by sin could not handle the wonders and weight of Glory. But we will be changed, and we will find ourselves and our Rest as made for each other.

Think about this: Holiness of heart and life just don't "fit in" here. A godly person is a stranger here (1 Peter 1:1) (If you "feel at home" here, that may be a dangerous sign.) But in Heaven, we will draw our holiness directly from God, as a spark from a flame, and we will be fully *at home* in our holiness ... for the first time in our experience.

All the gold and glory this world has to offer cannot bring rest to a follower of Jesus. They are of too little value. They feed only a part of who we are, but not all of who we are. The best this world gives does not suit a Jesus Follower. Having been redeemed at the high cost of the blood of Jesus, only being with Jesus will suit the Christian. We are not just animals. We are spiritual beings. We are made in God's Image. Only a Heaven with God fully present can suit our true nature. A Heaven without Jesus, even if full of physical pleasures, is impossible. It would be vile and beneath our created and redeemed dignity. But a Heaven where we know and rejoice in and with God moment by moment, for all eternity, suits our nature and God's purpose for us.

> *Now this is eternal life: that they know you, the only true God,*
> *and Jesus Christ, whom you have sent.*
> (John 17:3)

Now this is a good time to examine yourself. True, this side of Heaven we have mixed and corrupted desires. Part of us wants our sinful natures pleased – with sinful things - and part of us wants our redeemed natures pleased – with Jesus. But, ask yourself: "Do I find a growing desire for God in my heart?" "Am I increasingly dissatisfied with the best this world has to offer?" "Am I discovering that only Jesus and His Heaven can suit the 'me' God has made and redeemed me to be?" "Am I feeding my spirit and starving my flesh, or feeding my flesh and starving my spirit?"

The answers to these questions reveal the direction of your heart. The direction of your heart determines your destiny. Do not fool yourself! Heaven is about *being with the Lord* and if you do not want the Lord, then Heaven is not for you. But, if God, Father, Son, Holy Spirit, is your heart's desire, then God you shall have. It is about *holiness and freedom from sin*, and if that is your true desire, then you shall have it. This present life, for the Christian, is about hope, desire, and foretaste. Our Rest will be about certainty, fulfillment, and enjoyment. Then, and not before, you will find yourself finally "at home." You will be where your Treasure is, and your Rest will be perfectly suited – tailor-made – for you.

> *Take delight in the Lord,*
> *and he will give you the desires of your heart.*
> (Psalm 37:4)

So will it be with the resurrection of the dead. The body that is sown is perishable, it is raised imperishable; it is sown in dishonour, it is raised in glory; it is sown in weakness, it is raised in power, it is sown a natural body, it is raised a spiritual body.
If there is a natural body, there is also a spiritual body. ... And just as we have borne the image of the earthly man, so shall we bear the image of the heavenly man. (1 Corinthians 15:42-44;49)

8) God's provided Rest will be *Perfect and Complete.* Here, we have joy, but there is always sorrow nearby. We have some rest, but never without weariness of body or spirit. But in Heaven there will be no mixture of corruption with incorruption. There will be no waves in Heaven's harbour. In Heaven we will know the perfection of all for which God has purposed us, without any taint of sin. There will be day without night and sweetness without bitterness ... nothing to slight the fullness and completeness of what God has prepared for us.

It is hard to imagine a place with no sin whatsoever. We think sin is *normal,* but it is not! It is a corruption of our natures. We were created for holiness, not wickedness. Just as in a hospital sickness is *common* but not normal (health is normal but uncommon), so, in this life, sin is *common* but holiness is *normal.* In our Rest there will be no sin. Adam's sin will not be passed into Heaven, and our sin will not be known there. Here

we are saints who sin. There, we will be saints who do not sin!
The blood of Jesus, which already has removed the stain of sin
from our hearts will finish its work in presenting us spotless
and without fault before His Father's throne.

*To him who is able to keep you from stumbling and to present
you before his glorious presence without fault and with great
joy – to the only God our Saviour be glory, majesty, power and
authority, through Jesus Christ our Lord, before all ages, now and
for evermore! Amen.* (Jude 24,25)

I know you ... you would rather have a heart free from sin than
have all the world at your feet. You will! Right now, the battle
is on. You lie down to sleep, and here come those vile thoughts.
You rise to your day, you pray and read your Bible ... yet sin
and temptation follow your every step. Listen! These trials
and sins might follow you all the way to the grave – but they
will go no further! And then, sin will never trouble us again,
and ignorance, dullness, dimness, will be gone.

Right now, it is as if we are walking in the early morning light.
We see a bit, but there is so much we miss. It is so easy to
stumble! What would you give to have a perfect understanding
of truth? To have dark things enlightened? To have apparent
contradictions resolved? No more doctrinal controversies! No
more denominations and divides!   Our ignorance will be
corrected, our relationships will be resolved, our fractures
mended. How many of us here, in our mistaken zeal, have
caused more harm than good! In Heaven, Truth will shine like
the sun, in the very face of God. In a moment, we will be
enlightened. No more error. No more scandal.
Oh, for a day when pride, laziness, coldness of heart, mixed
motives, alloyed love, desire for place and power... Oh, for a
day when these are *gone*! That day is soon to come! We will

never again grieve the Spirit of God! There will never again be a word of gossip or even the slightest intent of it. No intrigue, no posturing, no hint of hypocrisy. Imagine relationships without a shadow of manipulation or selfishness. What a day!

As the full moon reflects nothing but the fullness of the sun, so shall our faces reflect nothing but the light of God, with nothing to eclipse the fullness. Our Rest will be Perfect and Complete.

May God himself, the God of peace, sanctify you through and through. May your whole spirit, soul and body be kept blameless at the coming of our Lord Jesus Christ. The one who calls you is faithful, and he will do it. (1 Thessalonians 5:23-24)

9) Our Rest will be a *Total Deliverance From Suffering.* Cause and effect. Sin the cause, suffering the effect. When the cause is gone, the effect will cease!

Oh, glorious day!

We will rest from the suffering of *doubt.* Doubts are like bad weeds growing in the good ground of a Christian's heart. One day soon they will be weeded out and gone forever. No more anguishing over unsolved mysteries and painful challenges to faith. No more need of endless apologetics (so useful and needful now). Sermons and signs, books and conferences, all aimed at confirming our faith, will be suddenly obsolete when love is in full fruit, and we see our wonderful Lord Jesus face to face. While we will certainly be forever learning and growing, we will not have a grain of doubt or unbelief mixed with our wonderful discoveries of God.

We will rest from the suffering of *fearing God's displeasure.* This is now so often the devil's tool! Now we suffer under this sense that somehow God is not happy with us. When we get to Heaven, we will no longer be in the desert of displeasure, but in the oasis of God's love. We will then see that while there were moments when - in love - He hid His face from our wicked hearts and actions, His heart for us was always good, and He always did and now does receive us with great joy in Jesus.

There will be no more suffering from *the temptations of Satan.* What a trial to a Christian to be constantly battling the urgings to deny his Lord Jesus! How wearisome the battle! Every true follower of Jesus knows temptation. Every soldier of Christ who refuses peace with the enemy knows the endless evil strategies of Satan to entice and lure into sin. We are tempted to distrust God's goodness, to undervalue Jesus and His Cross, to doubt the Bible, to argue with God's providential leading. We are tempted to embrace flat-out atheism, to entertain every sin of lust and sensuality, and to hate our brother. Our hearts are like powder kegs, ready to explode in sin as soon as one of Satan's sparks finds its way there.

Now, the shallow, casual church-goer, the one who just has a few Christian notions, does not know anything of this battle against temptation. But the earnest follower of Jesus, who guards and knows his own heart well, is all too acquainted with this war. Dear one! Do not give up this fight! Right now we walk amongst the snares and traps of our enemy. But we do not stand in our own strength, and Satan's temptations are not crimes for which we will be charged. And the day is coming when he will be bound up forever, and there will be no more missiles from him, for they cannot penetrate into God's Heaven. Soon this exhausting battle with temptation will be over - forever.

Even more, we will rest from *the temptations of the world and the flesh.* It is not only the devil who seeks to persuade us from following Jesus. The world around us, and our own hearts, place upon us an almost intolerable load of temptation. Our own five senses can be a trap. Every part of our bodies can snare us. People, friends as well as enemies, can entangle our hearts. The good things we do can tempt us to pride, the bad things, to stubborn self-defense.

We can hardly open our eyes without inviting in danger. If we look up to others, envy lurks, if down on others, contempt. Someone's bigger house can tempt us to covet, a smaller one, to arrogance. Beauty draws us to lust, ugliness to loathing.

Sometimes we can hardly hear a word without temptation slithering about us. Slander, cruel replies, foul-worded responses, coarse joking, spring up in our hearts before their sentences are even finished!

Do you think I am overstating things? Take time and really examine your heart, and you will see that I am understating things!

Look at our appetite, our pride of appearance (whether we love or hate how we look!), our intelligence, our constant looking for applause, our despising of others when *they* receive it, our parading of spirituality, our desire to be seen to be a humble servant of Jesus, our displaying of theological prowess and Bible knowledge, our temptation to argue ... especially about spiritual things, our undervaluing what God has given and gifted to us, despising our lot in ministry and life ... all proofs positive of our pride!

Should I stop?
What about our temptation to divide brothers and to see others fail? How quickly do we jump to judge others, to despise another's authority and to abuse ours? How strong is the urge to belittle another, to betray a confidence, to gossip, to name-

drop, to promote ourselves at the expense of another or even of Jesus and His Gospel!

Temptation!

Here ... with the world around us, our hearts within us, and Satan beside us ... the battle is never-ending. But there! In our Rest, temptation will be *gone forever*! Think of how much energy and ability we will have for God and good when we are no longer spending it in battling temptation.

In Heaven we will rest from the sufferings caused by *persecution and abuse at the hands of the wicked.* If your Christianity is at all genuine, then to one degree or another, you now suffer persecution, for "everyone who wants to live a godly life in Christ Jesus will be persecuted" (2 Timothy 3:12). Now you might not suffer as some, but being scorned, bypassed, ridiculed, ignored, or banished is painful enough, let alone being imprisoned and butchered. But the day is coming, and soon, when the prayers of the martyred, "How long O Lord until you avenge our blood?" (Revelation 5:10) will be answered and justice will be served.

Here our crown is one of pain, then of Glory. Now we are hated for Jesus and His Gospel; then we will be loved with all the saints in the presence of Jesus. Now some may mock, scorn, and torture while we weep, but soon they will weep in their damnation while we rejoice in our salvation. Now we are strangers in this fading world, but soon we will be at home in a world that never fades.

When God pulls the curtain on history, and this river of persecution – long polluted with the blood of Christians – is dried up; when we are called out of this wilderness and into the New Jerusalem, descended from Heaven; when mercy and justice begin to rule unhindered; *then* their raging and their fury will be silenced.

All the miserable laws written against the Gospel will be overturned in Heaven. The peoples who have suffered so will be glorified and their blood avenged. But now, be patient. Wear your sufferings as a crown. Be thankful for every small deliverance, but know that complete deliverance is coming. Our God is sure to:

... pay back trouble to those who trouble you and give relief to you who are troubled, and to us as well. This will happen when the Lord Jesus is revealed from heaven in blazing fire with his powerful angels. (2 Thessalonians 1:6,7)

And then, we will rest from the suffering caused by *divisions and conflicts amongst Christians.* Imagine! No denominations! Luther and Zwingli, Arminians and Calvinists, those of this position and that, perhaps proud of their particular point or discovery – all will be caught up with one another in the wonders of God. We will be reconciled and humbled before the perfections of the God who is greater than our opinions and limited earthly understanding.

How sad these divisions have been! How many bitter tears have we cried and biting words have we spoken! The suffering that brothers in Jesus experience when we are divided may be more painful than any suffering the world can inflict upon us. It is enough that the world is against us ... why have we added to it by being against one another? Satan has used our zeal and pride to grieve Jesus and hinder His cause. Today two walk together; tomorrow they may be locked in bitter dispute. God weeps while Satan laughs.

But a day is coming – what a happy day! – when there will be one God, one church, one heart, one joy-filled worship, forever. No more arguments about baptism, communion, music, church government, dress. No more pride of knowledge and ministry to separate Christian from Christian. No more discord, but only one great harmonious choir! There, when we will continually dwell together in unity, the Lord will – as we have never known here – bestow His fullest blessing (Psalm 133).

Then we will be freed from the suffering of *sharing in the trials of those we love.* As if we did not have enough of our own troubles, we suffer along with the sufferings of those we love. How many funerals, hospitals, houses of sorrow have we visited here? Hardly a week goes by without more sad news of a dear one being afflicted in some horrible way. The Church of Jesus is a hospital for sinners and the sick. The better the church, the worse the cases, and the greater the sufferings. Yes, there are moments of joy and shouts of victory, but there are many days of mourning and anguish. The Church of Jesus exists for the broken and dying. Let the country club exist for the frivolous. The Church is for the desperate.

Now we "mourn with those who mourn." How can we not weep and bleed with our brothers and sisters? Oh the weeping over those whose earthly suffering seems endless! But our Rest is coming when we will be free from all this. There will be no more fear of bad news. No more tragic diagnosis, family pain, tearful gatherings, homes rent by rebellion, coffins, and dirges. Rather, we will rejoice in the fullness and restoration of those for whom we once wept. Their restoration will be our joy. Everyone alive, free from suffering, whole, and glorified!

And, we today grieve not just for the physical pain we see in others, but (perhaps even more) for the spiritual pain we see all around. What a day when the wanderer is finally home! What a day when the persecuted Church shall be clothed in radiant joy! What a wonderful day when the backslidden Church is revived and restored! Stop and imagine the day when the Church from persecuted lands, from sin-hardened lands, from pleasure-drunk lands – the Church that sometimes brought us so much sorrow here – is presented to Jesus as His radiant, spotless Bride.

We will rest from *our personal sufferings.* There are basically two types of suffering for a Christian: "Natural" and "Supernatural." Natural sufferings are those which simply accompany life in this world. Christians are not exempt from these. "Supernatural" are those which come from the hand of our good God for reasons which He determines right. Now, many of us today are (wrongly) convinced that life is a pleasure cruise, with just a few stormy days thrown in. Many question the goodness of God when their pleasure cruise is interrupted. We need to read our Bibles! Life is a storm with a few calm days thrown in. And, to those who know and experience the reality of personal sufferings, whether originating from the normal course of life, or coming directly from the hand of God, the thought of a Rest from all sufferings, safe in Heaven's Harbour, is a source of great joy.

What fragile pots of dust we are! Every sense we have is an opening for sin and sorrow. Grief, fear, worry, disease seem to enter through every crack in our frail structure. Dangers abound and illness is always but a breath away. I know this sounds strange to those who are accustomed to a buffet of pleasure, but listen: There are many of us who can scarcely remember a day without some anguish visiting us. And, even if you are blessed with the sunshine of health today, all it takes is a microscopic creature, or a mosquito, or a careless driver to land you on a bed of suffering. In that day, what a joy it will be if you can anticipate your coming Rest, when all this suffering is over forever.

Dear one! A day of endless joy and peace is ahead. That weary, worn body of yours does not have long to go! Soon there will be no more toil and sweat, no more fevers and aches, no more wheelchairs and canes, no more masters and slaves, hunger and thirst, sleepless nights and exhausted days, frostbite and sunburn, sorrow, fear, weariness, and maddening pain. You who weep now will soon see the fruit of your faith. Soon you will see how God really has been absolutely faithful to you through all your treacherous journey in this land of sin and sadness. And, in seeing, joy will be yours forever.

They will enter Zion with singing; everlasting joy will crown their heads.
Gladness and joy will overtake them, and sorrow and sighing will flee away.
(Isaiah 35:9,10)

There is a rest coming from *the suffering of endless duty in a fallen world.* What a weight it can be to give your best, every day, and often in a thankless or difficult situation! What parent does not know the suffering of undying love, sleepless nights, constant praying, instructing, correcting, encouraging, protecting – often only to have their faithful labours thrown in the dirt and trampled upon? What about the toil of the Christian employee who is beyond diligent and honest, yet who is bypassed, perhaps mocked and scorned, and who suffers under the hand of a hard boss?

There is a day coming when the sweat and thorns that accompany toilsome duty in this life will be no more.

87

The pastor, that godly man (and his dear wife!) who weeps and watches and prays; who diligently studies and faithfully teaches; who day and night carries the burden of his charge on his heart; whose health is broken from the burden; and who withstands the mockings and taunts of so many who hate Jesus – soon his suffering for the faithful discharge of his duties will be forged into a crown!

The hard-working farmer, the soldier, the doctor, the policeman, the homemaker, the conscientious boss – soon their burdens will be gone and a garment of praise will be theirs.

What a wonderful Rest Heaven will be!

Finally, there will be rest from the suffering of *not being with God.* We have His Word, and His Spirit, and His Church, but how we ache to be with *Him.* We understand the poet's cry: "My soul thirsts for God, for the Living God. When can I go and meet with God?" (Psalm 42:2) We will never again have days when we seem distant from God. We will not have to look for our Treasure again. We won't ever look within and wonder why Jesus is not in our hearts. We won't need to find Him in bread and wine again, nor hunt for Him in the Bible. No more suffering the pain of absence from the One our hearts desire. No more lying in our beds or struggling through our days wondering where God is (Song of Songs 3:1,20) for He will "place us like a seal over His heart" (Song of Songs 8:6) and we will never be distant from Him again.

10) The last jewel in the crown of Heaven is this: *Our Rest is an Eternal, Unending Rest.* Here is the Jewel of all jewels, the Crown of all crowns. All of the other wonders of our Rest would be pointless if they were not eternal. If we had some sense that our temptations would one day return, or that our sufferings would show up again; if there was a fear that

perhaps in a millennia or two there would be a fee payable, or that we would grow unsuited for and bored with Heaven, then the sufferings of Jesus would be for nothing.

Death takes the shine out of every earthly delight. The fact that wonderful things are always and only temporary is never far from our thoughts. This present life loses significance if we are only creatures of time and not also of eternity. If our dreams are only for this age, then our dreams are too small and beneath the dignity of our nature. Death is an insult to who we are, for we are made in the very Image of the Eternal One, and deep inside we demand eternity.

Eternity! Stop and think about it. *Often.* Study it and ponder it until your perspective is transformed and put right. Let the fact of eternity cause you to put away the trifling idols which only distract you. Dream about eternity until you awake from your small, time-bound dreams. We will live and *never* die. We will rejoice in God's Infinite nature and presence forever and ever. How sweet are those two words "never" and "forever"!

What revives the weary heart like the news of our *eternal* Rest? If I will live forever, I will love forever. I will praise forever. I will glory forever. I will learn forever. I will be holy forever. I will be with all the redeemed forever. And ... best of all ... I will be with Jesus forever. Let the wonders of *that day* be a medicine for you *this day.* Jesus Himself will crown you with an eternal crown of righteousness which is taken from His own. Forever, with all Heaven we will sing:

Now unto the King eternal, immortal, invisible, the only wise God, be honour and glory for ever and ever. Amen.
(1 Timothy 1:17 KJV)

Well, I have tried to give you a glimpse of the glory that is coming. As surely as my words have fallen short, I can tell you, believer in Jesus, that my dim descriptions will very soon breakout in brightness over you. So, while we wait for that day, let's be about Jesus' business! Let's stir our hearts for the Gospel and run and fight and love knowing all the time what is before us. God is for us. All Heaven is watching. So, we dare not do disservice to our souls, to Jesus, to His Gospel, and to His Heaven - by dallying in this world when we should be pressing toward the one to come!

Scriptures to Ponder:

Therefore, my brothers and sisters, make every effort to confirm your calling and election. For if you do these things, you will never stumble, and you will receive a rich welcome into the eternal kingdom of our Lord and Saviour Jesus Christ. (2 Peter 1:10,11)

> *Yet this I call to mind*
> *and therefore I have hope:*
> *Because of the Lord's great love we are not consumed,*
> *for his compassions never fail.*
> *They are new every morning;*
> *great is your faithfulness.*
> (Lamentations 3:21-23)

> *Lord, you have been our dwelling-place*
> *throughout all generations.*
> *Before the mountains were born*
> *or you brought forth the whole world,*
> *from everlasting to everlasting you are God ....*
> *Satisfy us in the morning with your unfailing love,*
> *that we may sing for joy and be glad all our days.*
> (Psalm 90:1-3;14)

Questions to Consider:

1) If Heaven was purchased by your works, rather than Christ's blood, could you ever have an assurance of salvation?

2) Of all the wonders of our Rest spoken of above, which comforts you the most? What are you most looking forward to in Heaven?

3) Are you anticipating your Rest or loving this life too much?

4) How should a joyful anticipation of Heaven shape your life today?

Chapter Eight

Who Receives God's Rest?

Having gone a bit further past the curtain, discovering something of the wonders of Heaven, let's take just a brief moment to learn about those happy ones who will receive this Rest. Who are they? What have they done to deserve such a blessing?

When we look at God's Heaven, it is natural to assume that those who will inhabit such an amazing place must themselves be magnificent beings. In describing them – did we not know better – we would expect a trumpet fanfare and the sun itself bowing down in homage to them. But that is not what we find. Those who gain Heaven are far from magnificent in themselves. They appear as bags of dust. They are broken and lowly. They are frail and flawed creatures on a brief journey through time.

"Heaven? For them?"

When we watch their lives, we do not seem to see much of anything that would fit them for eternity in the presence of God! They are caught up in themselves and forgetful of God. They love themselves above all else – including the God who made them. They trust themselves. They admire themselves. They congratulate themselves. They crave the admiration of others and seek to draw attention away from God and to themselves. It seems as if each one would gladly be served and admired above anything or anyone else. Each one is his own little idol. Regarding these idols: Their bodies and minds decay, and then they drop into a grave.

"God's Heaven? For such as these?"

Believe it or not, these cracked and marred clay pots possess within the very image of God. They are actually living souls. Though deeply flawed by sin there is, nonetheless, something within them at odds with what we see on the surface: Deep down inside, they are divine image-bearers.

It is from *these* that we find those who will inhabit the wonders of God's Heaven!

From this vast crowd of idolatrous creatures, there is a company who have received a particular, undeserved mercy from God. God has gone to work on them, restoring them - though undeserving - to their original glory. In some ways they seem to be but a small part of this great lost throng we call mankind. In other ways, this gathering is larger and more glorious than we can imagine. From eternity past God has predestined them for an undeserved redemption through the blood of His Son. While "few" enter through that narrow gate (Matthew 7:13), this "few" is a "multitude" beyond number from "every tongue and nation" (Revelation 7:9) God has set His redeeming love upon them, that they might be fully recovered from their disastrous state, and brought to His Heaven, all "to the praise of His glorious grace" (Ephesians 1:6).

These who will inhabit Heaven have been purchased by the blood of God's Son. They will be kept by God's Son. None of them will ever perish, and no one can take them out of Jesus' grip. They are safe in Jesus. But, while God's grace toward them is beyond wonderful, they themselves have responded to God's love in such a way that they have set themselves apart from the rest of the world. While still imperfect – unfinished – they are deeply aware (1) of their own sin; (2) of their inability to cleanse themselves; (3) of the wonderful grace of God in Jesus to pay for their sin; (4) of their hatred of their sins; (5) of their daily pursuit of holiness of heart and life; and (6) of their total confidence in Jesus to save, keep, and present them faultless before their Father.

They are marked by their treasuring of Jesus, and not of this passing world. There is a hunger within them as they actively pursue God. They have made the daily choice to come away from sin and follow Jesus. There is a joy within them that the rest of humanity cannot understand, and a seriousness about eternity that is not found among those who are captivated by trivial things. Their conversation is different. Their use of time is different. Their hopes and dreams are different. They spend their money differently. They view death differently. They love one another. They love their enemies. They hold the things of this world loosely.

God's grace is clearly doing a remarkable work in them. He is preparing them for His Heaven! They are His "little flock" who need never be afraid, for His Father is pleased to give them His Kingdom (Luke 12:33).

Does this describe you? Are you a part of this happy company? Please, stop and look into your own heart and see if God is doing such a work in your life. Be sure. Assume nothing. Eternity is at stake.

Ask yourself:

"Do I see that I have been created by and for God, and that therefore every created thing is incapable of bringing me true happiness?" "Do I see that my own sin blocks my way to God and I am utterly cast upon Jesus to deal with my sin and bring me to His Father?" "Do I see that I have no hope besides Jesus Christ?" "Seeing that I have no hope but Jesus, have I cast down any notion of my own righteousness?" "And so, do I treasure Him supremely, as a merchant would the most costly gem in the world?" "And, treasuring Jesus, am I hating sin ... my sin ... and repenting as soon as sin is present?" "Do I hate sin more than I fear death?" "Though I do not love Him as I should, do I still want to love nothing else so much?" "Am I trusting Jesus to cleanse and keep me all the way to His Father's house, and have I covenanted with Him that He shall have the highest place in my heart?"

Do not fly over these questions! Your heart resonance with them is of highest importance to your eternal happiness. If your heart desires to say "yes" to these searching questions, (or at least wants to say "yes") then you can be sure that God is at work in you to save you through Jesus, and that you are a part of these happy "few," and that His Rest will be yours.

But I must warn you! If the words above seem strange to you, or if they grate against you, if they offend or weary you, then I pray that the Lord Jesus will have mercy upon you. I pray that the eyes of your heart may be opened to see your wickedness, your inability to save yourself, and Jesus' full sufficiency and readiness to receive you, if you will only come. Give up your resistance and surrender to the One who loves you with an everlasting love. Otherwise, you have no hope. Think about the end of your brief life here on earth and weigh it up against *eternity*. You have an opportunity now, but one day you will not. The price is paid, the Saviour's heart is open, and there is a willing God. The only obstacle is your proud, sinful self. Give yourself up to God! *You* can know this Rest that I am speaking of, and discover your bright inheritance with the people of God.

Scriptures to Ponder:

I keep asking that the God of our Lord Jesus Christ, the glorious Father, may give you the Spirit of wisdom and revelation, so that you may know him better. I pray that the eyes of your heart may be enlightened in order that you may know the hope to which he has called you, the riches of his glorious inheritance in his holy people, and his incomparably great power for us who believe. That power is the same as the mighty strength he exerted when he raised Christ from the dead and seated him at his right hand in the heavenly realms, far above all rule and authority, power and dominion, and every name that is invoked, not only in the present age but also in the one to come. (Ephesians 1:17-22)

Brothers and sisters, think of what you were when you were called. Not many of you were wise by human standards; not many were influential; not many were of noble birth. But God chose the foolish things of the world to shame the wise; God chose the weak things of the world to shame the strong. God chose the lowly things of this world and the despised things – and the things that are not – to nullify the things that are, so that no one may boast before him. It is because of him that you are in Christ Jesus, who has become for us wisdom from God – that is, our righteousness, holiness and redemption. (1 Corinthians 1:26-30)

Questions to Consider:

1) If Heaven is not for the magnificent but for the meek, what does say to you about the character of God?

2) When you carefully examine your heart, do you find a total reliance upon Jesus and His saving grace, or are you in any way relying upon yourself for salvation?

3) If our Rest is something *received* instead of *achieved,* what does this say to you when you are at your lowest? How does this give you a welcome message for broken people?

Chapter Nine

Six Truths About Heaven Proven by the Bible

Dear Friend, I hope you do not think yourself more knowledgeable than the Bible. Why? Because if you are going to be *sure* about Heaven, you have to humble yourself and accept that the Bible knows more than you do, that it is true, that Jesus really is the Son of God, and that the entire Gospel enterprise is true and reliable. Otherwise, you are left to your own ideas.

Everything in this book is built upon what the Bible says about things that really matter. These are not my ideas, nor the ideas of any man or council of men. So, I hope you take them as true because the Bible says so, and in doing so, that they will be of profound benefit to your soul.

I want here to present six truths about our Rest that we can be sure of – because the Bible says so.

1) Our Rest is *foreordained by God for us and we are foreordained by God for it.* The whole plan of Heaven has been ordered in the eternal councils of God, the Father, the Son, and the Holy Spirit. The entire salvation history is not "Plan B" but eternally purposed by God. God did not say "oops" when we went bad. He had and has a plan. That plan is the Eternal Gospel and it involves Heaven and His Redeemed People.

The Scriptures that prove this are too many for this little book. Here are just a few:

...God is not ashamed to be called their God, for he has prepared a city for them. (Hebrews 11:16)

> *'What no eye has seen,*
> *what no ear has heard,*
> *and what no human mind has conceived' –*
> *the things God has prepared for those who love him –*
> (1 Corinthians 2:9)

...God chose you as firstfruits to be saved through the sanctifying work of the Spirit and through belief in the truth. (2 Thessalonians 2:13)

And those he predestined, he also called; those he called, he also justified; those he justified, he also glorified. (Romans 8:30)

So, I'll ask you: Who can rob God's people of that which God has eternally purposed for them?

2) *We are redeemed from slavery to sin specifically for this Rest.* We have already seen that Heaven has been purchased by Jesus for us. But I want to make sure that we also see that we have been purchased for Heaven by Jesus. Another way to say this is: We have been redeemed from sin. And that redemption was at great cost, not to ourselves, but to Jesus:

For you know that it was not with perishable things such as silver or gold that you were redeemed from the empty way of life handed down to you from your ancestors, but with the precious blood of Christ, a lamb without blemish or defect. (1 Peter 1:18,19)

... we have confidence to enter the Most Holy Place by the blood of Jesus ... (Hebrews 10:19)

Since Jesus has redeemed us for Heaven by His blood, Heaven is secured for us and us for it. Either Jesus' blood is wasted, or our redemption is sure and certain!

3) As our redemption is purchased for us, *so it is promised to us.* Jesus Himself has told us that He wants us with Him in Heaven. He prayed for this on the last night of His earthly life. Do you think His Father will answer His prayer? Yes!

Father, I want those you have given me to be with me where I am, and to see my glory, the glory you have given me because you loved me before the creation of the world. (John 17:24)

More, Jesus did not just promise *us* that He will secure us for Heaven (John 3:16), He promised *His Father* that He would secure us for Heaven!

All those the Father gives me will come to me, and whoever comes to me I will never drive away. For I have come down from heaven not to do my will but to do the will of him who sent me. And this is the will of him who sent me, that I shall lose none of all those he has given me, but raise them up at the last day. For my Father's will is that everyone who looks to the Son and believes in him shall have eternal life, and I will raise them up at the last day. (John 6:37-40)

Hallelujah! Our salvation is as secure as the very promise of Jesus to His Father!

4) *The unending grace of God, shown in endless ways, gives constant testimony to the fact and future of Heaven.* God is not a wasteful God! Stop and think about all the offerings of His grace to you: the endless times He has recalled and restored you; the small and the great ways that He has and is proving

His preserving love to you. Is this all for nothing? Is God pouring His love and care upon you lavishly for no reason? Does this not point to an end which He has in mind?

Would God have encouraged us to watch and pray, given us His Word and His Spirit, commanded us to repent, to believe, to knock and seek, to run and fight, all for no purpose? Where do these desires come from? Yourself? Really? Are *you* that holy? The willingness and drive come from God. He has a great design for us – Heaven with Him.

Where does the ability to suffer and persevere come from? Ourselves? This ability to keep going is evident proof that God has a purpose for us that transcends this brief life – Heaven!

And God is able to make all grace abound toward you; that ye, always having all sufficiency in all things, may abound to every good work. (2 Corinthians 9:8 KJV)

The Lord will rescue me from every evil attack and will bring me safely to his heavenly kingdom. To him be glory for ever and ever. (2 Timothy 4:18)

5) The Bible tells us that *God has already given us – now – a foretaste of the feast which He is preparing for us.* Is God cruel? Does He tease us? Will He give us the appetizer but not the main course? Will He awaken a hunger only to leave us wanting?

These inner stirrings, those moments of joy, the times when we can sense Heaven ahead: Are these not early promises of certain blessings to come? Do they originate with you? No! They are tokens from a good God of what is ahead. Just like the smell of bread from the kitchen is an awakening promise of

John D. Gillespie

what is sure to come, so God in many ways gives us a "whiff" of what is ahead.

So Jesus tells us that even now:

Neither shall they say, Lo here! or, lo there! for, behold, the kingdom of God is within you. (Luke 17:21 KJV)

And Peter can say:

Though you have not seen him, you love him; and even though you do not see him now, you believe in him and are filled with an inexpressible and glorious joy, for you are receiving the end result of your faith, the salvation of your souls. (1 Peter 1:8,9)

And Paul tells us that our present possession of God's Holy Spirit (the Author of every spiritual desire we now have) is:

a seal ... a deposit guaranteeing our inheritance until the redemption of those who are God's possession – to the praise of his glory. (Ephesians 1:13,14)

6) Finally, the Bible *actually names people who entered their Rest.* Abraham, Lazarus, Enoch, the dying thief. Were they better than we are? No. If there is a Rest for them, there is a Rest for us. Sinners enter the Rest (that is why it is *Rest!*) by the unmerited favour of God. We can take courage from the Bible's proof that God has saved and will save those no better than we who put their trust in Him.

In bringing many sons and daughters to glory, it was fitting that God, for whom and through whom everything exists, should make the pioneer of their salvation perfect through what he suffered. Both the one who makes people holy and those who are

102

made holy are of the same family. So Jesus is not ashamed to call them brothers and sisters. He says,

> *'I will declare your name to my brothers and sisters;*
> *in the assembly I will sing your praises.'*
> (Hebrews 2:10-12)

The Bible is given to us from God to guide us and lead us heavenward. Without it, we are left to either our own musings or to flat out deception from Satan. Without the Bible we will become weird, worldly, or wicked - or some combination of all three – even as we are aspiring to Heaven. The Bible is as important to Heaven as a road is to a destination ... you cannot find a sure way to your Rest without it.

Scriptures to Ponder:

... He did this to make the riches of his glory known to the objects of his mercy, whom he prepared in advance for glory ... (Romans 9:23)

> *... with your blood you purchased for God*
> *persons from every tribe and language and people and nation.*
> *You have made them to be a kingdom and priests to serve our*
> *God, and they will reign on the earth.*
> (Revelation 5:9,10)

Do not be afraid, little flock, for your Father has been pleased to give you the kingdom. ... And I confer on you a kingdom, just as my Father conferred one on me, so that you may eat and drink at my table in my kingdom and sit on thrones, judging the twelve tribes of Israel. (Luke 12:32; 22:29-30)

Questions to Consider:

1) What are some "foretastes" of Heaven you have received?

2) Are you rejoicing in the promise of a prepared Rest? Do you think it too good to be true, or are you willing to rest your opinion about Heaven on what the Bible has to say about it?

3) How does understanding that the entire Gospel story is not "Plan B" but God's eternally purposed plan impact your assurance that God is actually at work in the details of your life?

Chapter Ten

Why Can't We Have Heaven Now?

Why do we have to wait? If God loves us so much, why do we have to travel through this valley of sorrow and trial?

First, *it is God's will that we should wait for our Rest.* He made us. He knows what is best for us. He can do what He wants, because He is sovereign, and what He wants is always best because He is good. Just as He has ordered that we do not have spring and harvest without winter, so He has ordered that we do not have Heaven without earth.

But it is easy to see reasons for God's wise ordering of this. Waiting for Heaven, growing in Christlikeness over the course of this life as God prepares us for Heaven, is in keeping with the way we see God working all around us. God works in the small things the way He is working in the big thing. God's normal way is to work gradually. The strong man is first a weak child. The scholar is first the infant learning his letters. The tall oak was once an acorn. The artist was once drawing stick-figures. We see God working this way every day in the ordinary. It is perfectly reasonable to expect Him to work this way in the extraordinary. He *prepares* us for our Rest.

Next, *it enhances God's grace and glory to bring us gradually to our Rest.* Let me try to explain. We are living in a fallen, broken, rebellious world. Yet it is precisely within this context that God is able to display endless graces and mercies that He will not have to display in Heaven. His amazing providential working, His weaving together in wisdom the rich tapestry of His power and purpose – in the midst of an all-out war – magnifies and displays His goodness and power in a way that

105

Heaven will not need and therefore not permit. If Adam had not been allowed to fall, then there would never have been cause for the wonders of the Gospel: God's mercies would have been locked up within Himself (and therefore unknown) forever! And, if He transported a believer to Heaven the moment he came to trust in Jesus, then God's continued mercy, wisdom, and power, His endless grace and patience, would likewise be locked away and unknown to us.

And, *it is for our good that God makes us wait for our Rest.* The difficulty of the journey will cause us to adore the wonders of the destination all the more. If it were not for trials and tribulations, we would easily forget God. It is invariably through conflict that we discover more and more of the wonders and goodness of God. His faithfulness is revealed in the storms as surely as on the sunny days. Perhaps more! Our love is refined, our faith is proven, our hearts are weaned from the trivial and our hunger for Jesus and His Heaven is enhanced by our having to wait.

How could the sweetness of Jesus, displayed in such an invitation as "Come to me, all you who are weary and burdened, and I will give you rest," (Matthew 11:28) mean anything, and contribute to the preciousness of Jesus and His Rest, if we did not have to take this troubled journey to Heaven?

God knows exactly what He is doing. Heaven will be all the sweeter because we have endured the bitterness of a long and dangerous journey through a barren land. What would Jesus' promises and consolations be if we had never experienced the tragedies and tears of this fallen world? All His invitations to the weary, all His promises of recovery and welcome, are meaningless in a trouble-free world. When we get to the end of our pilgrim journey, knowing that our days as strangers and sojourners are *over*, how wonderful and welcome will be our Rest!

We are now incapable of enjoying Jesus' Heaven. We love sin too much! Our hearts are divided! The world still fascinates too often. Remembering that it is God's normal way to work gradually, through providences, we need to get to that place where we are weary of this world – even of its best. This takes time. We are difficult projects! We need to get to where we are ready to be enraptured by Jesus because we are through with everything else. It is a mercy when one wearies of all his toys and gadgets and longs for more. What is Heaven if it is not rejoicing in the unmixed knowledge of God? How can we, who now pursue Him so little and love Him so coldly, fit into such a place where He is all in all? What is Heaven if it is not freedom from sin and self? How can we who love sin and self so much fit into a place where they are non-existent? I know that God sometimes, in His wisdom, suddenly takes a child of grace home, but His normal way is to work and work on us until we are through with temporal foolishness and hungry for what is solid and sure.

More, *our bodies, as they are now, cannot inhabit Glory.* We could not live right now in a constant state of heavenly revival. We would exhaust ourselves. As marvelous as our bodies are, they must be made like His in glory if they are to be fit for Heaven. Presently, they are too sick, too weak, too weary. They require too much care and repair. If our happy employment will be to worship, grow, and engage with God without interruption, our bodies are going to have to be glorified! So, we wait for a day when God "will transform our lowly bodies so that they will be like his glorious body" (Philippians 3:21).

Then, *we need to become weary of this world before we will truly value the next.* I am not here speaking of the trials of this world, but of its blessings. Foolish people believe that just a bit more of what this world has to offer will finally bring them the rest for which they long. But wiser souls know that in the end the best this world has to offer leaves one empty and looking for something beyond. Wiser souls see that more of this world actually increases weariness and care. It does not reduce it. Remember Solomon? He had all that this world could ever offer him ... and the result? "So I hated life ... All of it is meaningless, a chasing after the wind. I hated all the things I had toiled for under the sun ..." (Ecclesiastes 2:17,18).

Heaven will be all the sweeter when the Lord has taken down all of our idols, reduced us to Himself, and shown us the vanity of trusting any finite thing – even the best – to fill the infinite void within us.

And, *God has not prepared this present age, but another, for us to fully know Him.* It is not here that He has established His throne. It is not here that he has fully pulled back the curtain that we might behold His glory (John 17:24; Psalm 27:4). Here God gives us tokens of His love; He gives us tastes of His banquet, glimpses of His Glory, and moments of His presence, but He has reserved the fullness for Heaven. We need to accept and understand this or we will be forever frustrated. There is a distance right now that will be closed one day. But for now, how can anyone who has made the Lord his treasure be fully at Rest and satisfied while there is a distance between them?

Finally, *we are not yet ready to receive Heaven's glories.* Understand this: True, the entire Gospel world is a world of grace, and not of works. But grace does not mean there are no treasures to find and rewards to earn. The Bible speaks of crowns and prizes and cities. Today there are works to do and battles to fight. Tomorrow there is a joy to enter into and a kingdom to inherit.

Are you ready *now* for a crown of righteousness? Have you already finished your good fight? Have you kept the faith and run the race until its end? You know better! You know there are still battles to fight and laps to run. You know, as you examine your own heart, that there is still so much work for grace to do in you before you are ready for all that God has laid up for you! You know that there are still works prepared by God for you to do.

God has His Rest awaiting you, but it is not time yet. You will know when you have "fought the good fight ... finished the race ... kept the faith" (2 Timothy 4:7). Then, and not a moment too soon or too late, His Rest will be yours.

So, we see why our Rest awaits us, and is not yet fully ours. Be careful, friend, that you do not complain against God while you wait for Heaven! Lament your own heart for God if you need to, but not God's for you! Don't expect a true Rest here and now, not from your wife, your money, or even your God. It is *ahead;* it is *to come.* Be busy with the Gospel, and keep your eyes on the prize.

Scriptures to Ponder:

They preached the gospel in that city and won a large number of disciples. Then they returned to Lystra, Iconium and Antioch, strengthening the disciples and encouraging them to remain true to the faith. 'We must go through many hardships to enter the kingdom of God,' they said. (Acts 14:21,22)

109

In all this you greatly rejoice, though now for a little while you may have had to suffer grief in all kinds of trials. These have come so that the proven genuineness of your faith – of greater worth than gold, which perishes even though refined by fire – may result in praise, glory and honour when Jesus Christ is revealed. Though you have not seen him, you love him; and even though you do not see him now, you believe in him and are filled with an inexpressible and glorious joy ... (1 Peter 1:6-8)

Questions to Consider:

1) Why is it important that we understand both the "now" and "not yet" of our salvation? Both the nearness and the distance of the Kingdom?

2) Do we understand that Heaven will be forever enhanced by God making us wait for it?

3) In what ways are you discovering that the finite cannot fill the void for the infinite with our hearts?

Chapter Eleven

Will Our Spirits Enjoy This Rest Before Our Bodies are Resurrected?

What will it be like the moment we die? What can we expect to experience? Does the Bible give us enough data to have any real understanding, or do we just have to guess? Some sects teach that our souls will sleep until our bodies are raised. Are they correct, or will we know and enjoy Jesus the moment we die in ways unknown here?

First, we need to agree that the Bible promises the resurrection of our bodies. God likes our bodies! He made them and called them "good" (Genesis 1:31). He is not going to give up on them, but He is going to redeem them. He is not going to say to Satan, "You can have their bodies, I will be content with their spirits." No, God is going to have it all!

But our citizenship is in heaven. And we eagerly await a Saviour from there, the Lord Jesus Christ, who, by the power that enables him to bring everything under his control, will transform our lowly bodies so that they will be like his glorious body. (Philippians 3:20-21)

Then, we need to agree that the moment we, as believers in Jesus, die, that our spirits are with the Lord:

We are confident, I say, and willing rather to be absent from the body, and to be present with the Lord ... And Jesus said unto him, Verily I say unto thee, Today shalt thou be with me in paradise ... having a desire to depart, and to be with Christ; which is far better ... (2 Corinthians 5:8; Luke 23:43; Philippians 1:23 KJV)

So, the question is, before we receive our resurrected bodies, will we be in our Rest, with the Lord, knowing and rejoicing in Him?

Without question, the Bible teaches that we will be in the wonderful presence of Jesus the very moment we die. Paul certainly knew and loved and enjoyed Jesus by faith while he was in this life. But he wanted, desired, hungered to be away from this life and to actually be with Jesus. He was sure that the moment he died, he would be "present with the Lord." Likewise, Jesus told us of a poor beggar named Lazarus, who, upon the death of his body, was in Paradise (Luke 16:23. The term "Abraham's bosom" was a Hebraism for "paradise.") Revelation looks into Heaven and sees there the "dead that die in the Lord ..." and tells us that they are at "rest from their labours" (Revelation 14:13 KJV). And, Hebrews refers to Heaven as the City of the Living God, where "the spirits of just men" have been "made perfect" (Hebrews 12:22,23 KJV).

Even more, the Bible tells us of Enoch and Elijah being already taken up to Heaven. Peter, James, and John see Moses – who has already died – on the Mount of Transfiguration. The dying Stephen knows that Jesus will receive his soul. Obviously, if the Lord Jesus will receive it, it is neither dead nor asleep! So the Bible assures us that knowing God (which we have begun to do here) *is* eternal life (John 17:3), and that whoever believes in Jesus *has* eternal life (John 3:36), and that if we "eat this bread" (that is, believe in Jesus), we will live forever (John 6:51). Since it is clear that eternal life is nothing less than being with Jesus, doesn't it makes sense to see that if we are not immediately with the Lord, even before the resurrection of our bodies, but have to "wait" perhaps thousands of years in some strange state of "soul sleep," then this is not eternal life – in any meaningful way - at all? (When the New Testament speaks of a believer being "asleep" in Jesus (Acts 7:60) it is simply a figure of speech for them having died. (John 11:11-14)

Remember when Paul had his amazing vision of Heaven (2 Corinthians 12)? He tells us that he was caught up to the highest ("third") Heaven. He tells us that he did not know if he was in his body or out of it. This tells us that the spirit alone, even without the body, is capable of beholding and experiencing Heaven. Remember when Jesus told us not to be afraid of persecutors who can kill our bodies but not our souls (Matthew 10:28)? Certainly, this tells us that when evil men have killed our bodies – separated our bodies from our souls – our souls have *not* been killed. They are still alive! God has breathed His life into us (Genesis 2:7). We are not just animals, but we are living souls – something not said of any other creature God has created.

Dear believer! Know, to your great comfort, that the moment your spirit leaves your body, you will be with the Lord. Yes, your body will one day be raised in glory, but you ... *you* ... will know a warm welcome home the moment you breathe your last. No sooner will you cast off this old flesh then you will be with Jesus, and with the countless dear ones who have preceded you, their spirits now made perfect, and with the very angels of God.

Hallelujah!

Scriptures to Rejoice In:

I know a man in Christ who fourteen years ago was caught up to the third heaven. Whether it was in the body or out of the body I do not know – God knows. And I know that this man – whether in the body or apart from the body I do not know, but God

113

knows – was caught up to paradise and heard inexpressible things, things that no one is permitted to tell ... (2 Corinthians 12:2-4)

When the members of the Sanhedrin heard this, they were furious and gnashed their teeth at him. But Stephen, full of the Holy Spirit, looked up to heaven and saw the glory of God, and Jesus standing at the right hand of God. 'Look,' he said, 'I see heaven open and the Son of Man standing at the right hand of God.'
At this they covered their ears and, yelling at the top of their voices, they all rushed at him, dragged him out of the city and began to stone him. Meanwhile, the witnesses laid their coats at the feet of a young man named Saul.
While they were stoning him, Stephen prayed, 'Lord Jesus, receive my spirit.' (Acts 7:54-59)

Questions to Consider:

1) What comfort do you receive from the knowledge that very soon you will be with Jesus?

2) While the great joy of Heaven will be being with the Lord, are you considering the wonder of meeting those who have preceded you to their Rest?

3) How should this hope of immediate joy upon death motivate you today toward holiness and perseverance?

Chapter Twelve

It Is Our Privilege to Help Others Toward Heaven

God has given us the most wonderful Treasure imaginable: Himself and His Heaven. This is our Rest. It is not possible to imagine anything, ever, more blessed than our Rest.

So, the question is obvious: Why are we so slow to help others to enter God's Rest? Think with me: Those around us do not see the wonders of Heaven. We are beginning to. They do not see the horrors of Hell: We see something of them. We can see them wandering toward destruction: They are insensible to it. And still, for all that we see and they do not, we will hardly ever stir ourselves to love them enough to *speak* of eternal realities. How few Christians set out with deliberate intention to see souls saved!

In this chapter we will take an interlude from our discovery of Heaven and will try to press upon ourselves the privilege and duty we have to share Jesus with others.

1) *Our hearts must be moved by the misery of our fellows' souls.* Pray and ask God to fill you with love and compassion for the lost! God will bless our labours if we will but earnestly desire the conversion of others and set our hearts to the work. We need to *take opportunities,* with an aim to God being glorified in others coming to Jesus. Our motive is not our fame, but God's, and their eternal happiness.

Jesus was often moved to compassion and felt love for lost people (Mark 10:21; Mark 8:2; Matthew 9:36). He spoke of God's the Fathers heart of compassion for the wasteful wanderer (Luke 15:20). He told us that He came to seek and

115

save the lost (Luke 19:10). Shouldn't we pray and seek a heart like our Saviour's? We are obedient to Jesus when we have tender hearts of compassion for others' souls. We are disobedient to Jesus when we allow ourselves to be hard-hearted. When we would rather scold than share Good News, we are not walking as Jesus walked!

Brothers and sisters! What a joy it is to obey Jesus and to walk as He walked! We need to get on with the work of evangelism, and not delay any longer. Perhaps the lost delay *coming* to Christ because we delay *going* to them! Delay is disobedience, both for them and for us. Our delaying betrays our heart trouble. It actually speaks of a lack of love, not just for the lost, but for Jesus. While we delay, their roots go deeper into sin, and their malady moves toward an incurable infection. How many perish while we discuss evangelism!

It is no use arguing that a sinner's salvation is the sovereign work of God, so we need not be bothered about it. Yes, God alone is able to change a heart, but He uses us as a part of that change! We come with the message that He uses.

2) *We need to come in love, with hearts of compassion, and perhaps even with tears.* We will not win people to Jesus by scolding them, or by adopting some moral high ground over them. We will not shame them into the Kingdom! Let a man's enemies shame and scold; let us love and weep! Lost people need to see and even feel our love for them. They need to see beyond any doubt that the desire of our hearts toward them is to do them good, that we have no other motive than their blessing and God's glory.

3) *Our words need to be plain and earnest.* There is no time to play games. When the subject is deep and serious we dare not be shallow and trivial. People will see right through that. If

situations are grave, tell others plainly. Tell them humbly, but do not skirt the issue, any more than a faithful doctor will dance around a deadly diagnosis. Beware of committing deadly spiritual malpractice. Do not give false hope! Warn, plead, present. Speak of Christ and His Gospel with the confidence of a doctor with a sure remedy for a deadly disease. "Faithful are the wounds of a friend ... " (Proverbs 27:6 KJV).

Sometimes you need to call loudly to awaken one who is fast asleep. Even so, with those dead in sin, or comatose in their hearts, we need to be especially earnest. They need to know that we are not talking about sports or entertainment or even money. We are speaking with them about their souls and their eternity. We must labour to help them see that there is great danger in joking about Heaven and Hell, salvation and damnation. Their issue is grave. *Our earnestness* will affect *their earnestness*. If we are not zealous for their souls, we cannot expect them to be!

Those who are careless with their souls need to be reminded – by *us* – that time is moving quickly and this world and its pleasures will soon be gone. The honours of men will one day soon count for nothing. What profits us now will not profit us then. Just as surely as there is a Heaven, there is a Hell. God is just and judgment is coming ... What a great and terrible day that will be! Our friends need to see that they have spent too much time in their sin. While they have loitered, God has been profoundly patient. They have all this time grown harder and harder toward God and gone further and further from God.

Their situation is drastic!

They need to see that Jesus has shed His blood for them - for their sins. Mercy is available. People are praying, you are pleading, the Holy Spirit is prompting, and Heaven is *open*. But time is short, and Satan is waiting to claim them as his own. Ask them if they would really rather lose Heaven and have Hell all over their momentary pleasures. Plead with them to *think* about this!

This is the way we need to deal with sinners. But our unwillingness to have men dislike us actually serves to contribute to their damnation. I have to tell you to my shame and sorrow that I often have failed here. The words I have written are actually convicting me. May the Lord Jesus not hold this against me!

4) *Yet we must be wise.* "The fruit of the righteous is a tree of life; and he that winneth souls is wise." (Proverbs 11:30 KJV). The plow will break the ground when the ground is soft. There are right seasons and there are wrong seasons. To try to persuade one to Christ at the wrong time, to be unwise in your approach, is to squander pearls. Offering Jesus when someone is drunk might lead to a fight. In public could lead to disgrace. The right medicine given at the wrong time can harm the sick, and a wise doctor knows the right time. Being faithful in our privilege to witness Jesus to sinners requires that we prayerfully move when God gives the opportunities. Harvesting apples is good ... but not in the spring! Likewise, be wise and aware of the temperament of each person. Some require great gentleness; others can handle, and may even need, a firm hand and manner. Trust the Holy Spirit to give you wisdom! Ask Him for the right expressions, words to use, questions to ask.

The most precious, beautiful thing – the Gospel – offered in the wrong way, at the wrong time, and without love, will be taken to be an offensive and hideous monster, even though it is the very Truth of God.

5) *Speak with the authority of God.* It is vital that people know that you are not just giving your ideas and opinions. Make sure your friends understand that *you* believe you are speaking with the very authority of God. What good are *our* ideas where salvation is concerned? Let them reject our ideas and forget our names. What difference will that make? But God bears His own authority. Use Bible stories rather than your own. Tell them of the thief on the cross, the rich fool, the Pharisee and the tax collector. Don't be afraid to say, "God says in His Word ...." The Holy Spirit will own the authority of His Word and work miracles in hearts, but He does not have to own anything you say off the top of your own head!

6) *Stay on course until your aim is reached.* Satan and sinners will want you to become distracted, to lose your way, to follow some other trail to nowhere. Know where you are going. Stick to the issue. Discipline yourself! If you are dealing with a sin issue in your friend, do not wander off the topic! Be as precise and focused as a physician with a patient or a prosecutor with a jury. If you are trying to bring him to repentance, or to a change of behavior, do not move on to something else (he will want you to!) until he sees clearly what you are presenting to him and agrees to your terms! But mostly, remember that your aim is to bring him to a place where he sees his desperate need of Jesus and His Gospel. Keep that issue forefront. Do not allow yourself to be drawn away from this and down some cul-de-sac of controversy.

7) *Make sure that your life backs up your words.* There is not a greater witness for Jesus than a person whose life lines up with his or her words. There is scarcely a worse witness than a person whose life is at odds with his words. Show by your life that there is a genuine difference in your values, aims, and treasures. No, they do not need to see that you are "perfect,"

119

because you are not. But they do need to see that the Heaven you are persuading them to is in fact *your* aim, and that Jesus really is *your* Hope and Joy.

People can spot hypocrisy in an instant. If you speak ill of others, if you love money more than Jesus, if you are dishonest in small things, your friends will see it. Your witness will be ruined. If you are exhorting them to be humble while you are proud, to be pure while you are vile, to be tender while you are hard, your efforts will do far more damage than good. But! The steadiness of a holy, Jesus-centred life is a powerful message to unbelievers and a mighty weapon for good in God's hands.

8) *Encourage them toward the company of other Christians.* Bringing unbelievers into friendship with godly men and women will encourage them toward friendship with God. Help them see that *you* love the Body of Christ, His Bride, His Flock. Being with Christians will help them to rethink prejudices and wrong notions they have picked up regarding believers. Bring them with you to hear the Gospel taught and preached. Don't tell them to "go to church." Rather, invite them with you to the Church.

Be careful that you do not moan and complain about other Christians in their presence (don't do it at all!). Avoid displaying a divisive, proud attitude toward other churches – this will only feed their pre-conceived notions about what Christians are like. Accompany them to warm and winsome meetings where the Word is opened to our hearts, where Heaven is opened to our prayers, and where we are opened to one another.

Finally: *Don't give up!* You may not see them come to Christ the first time you speak with them (most likely, they will not).

Follow after them! If they are not pursued with the warm love of Jesus, they will soon grow cold. Wear them out with love! Do not let them rest in their sins. Most will not be saved from sin's entanglements without persistent, diligent work - from you and others in partnership with God.

But, dear friends, seeing that it is our happy privilege and solemn duty to share Jesus and His Gospel with those who have yet to know Him, and to be diligent, wise, and bold in our pursuit of the lost, is it not a strange wonder that we rarely find a Christian among us who sets about to do this with all his heart? Why?

1) *Our own Gospel poverty hinders us.* Many of us have not sufficiently seen the Treasure that is Jesus. We have not truly tasted of the Feast that is the Gospel of Grace. So, how can we passionately draw others to it? More than that, having not seen or tasted, we are still loving our sins too much to even consider reaching out to the lost. Many of us are to some degree guilty of the very same sins which we see in those around us. We may not be actually committing adultery, but we have lurid hearts. We may not actually rob others, but we covet what they have. Our own poverty leads us to question things we should be sure of, like the eternal misery of our neighbours and the impending judgment of God. We "believe" the Scriptures like we "believe" a weather forecast. Their promise of judgment and Hell do not move us to action, but they bounce off our casual, careless hearts.

Were we rich in the Gospel, our unbelieving friends would reap the benefit for all eternity.

2) *We don't love others enough.* Just like the priest and the Levite passed by the wounded man, so we pass by those on

their way to Hell. Misery attracts compassion. They are on their way to eternal misery but where is our compassion? Think with me: Suppose your friend has fallen into a pit. Wouldn't it be strange if you passed right by without offering help? Even if you stopped and prayed but offered not your hand, could not he, and everyone else, bring a rightful charge of selfishness against you? Would he think you loved him? Now, here are our neighbours. They eat with us. They work with us. We see them everyday. They are either miserable now, or will be soon. Yet we say little or nothing to them about things that *matter*: Jesus, Heaven, Hell, salvation, their souls. Don't be surprised if they one day will bring a charge of loveless hypocrisy against us, for, "If anyone ... sees a brother or sister in need but has no pity on them, how can the love of God be in that person?" (1 John 3:17)

3) Another hindrance is *our sinful desire to please others.* We want to be popular more than we want to be faithful to God or helpful to people. We hate the thought of displeasing someone! This desire to be liked is, in fact, a terrible and subtle form of idolatry. Are we servants of Jesus or pleasers of men? We cannot be both (Galatians 1:10)! Can you imagine the case against a doctor who let a man die because he did not want to upset or offend him with bad news?

A desire to please others can be displayed in bashfulness. Bashfulness is actually a sin if it originates in a fear of others and a desire to make sure they are happy with us. We tend to think that shyness is an expression of humility, when if fact it is rooted in a desire to please others and is a close cousin of pride. It can cause us to be silent about Jesus when we should be speaking.

Dear ones! Let us seek grace to be obedient to Jesus, that we might be delivered from the crippling idolatry which loves the praise of men more than the praise of God.

4) And then we have *impatience.* Imagine if God had been as impatient with us as we often are with others! Soul-winning is hard work. There are many battles and many setbacks. We can lose friends and gain enemies. Who wants that? There are long periods of seemingly fruitless labour, and times when it seems that the harvest is ready, and a sudden storm destroys it and all of our work. It is easy to become cynical or bitter. It is then that remembering the patience of God (and others) towards us gives us the perspective and encouragement needed to not grow weary in this good work.

5) *Being too concerned about ourselves* keeps us from seeking the salvation of others. We foolishly think that the road to happiness is found in enhancing our own self-interests. Evangelism gets in the way of what *I* want to do! And yet, there is scarcely any tonic for the soul, any joy-giver for the heart, like earnestly sharing Jesus with another. Think about this, and you will agree with me: All the church committees, practices, ordinances, events, cannot bring you as much simple satisfaction and joy as opening your heart to a poor friend and sharing Jesus.

True? Yes!

Imagine this scene with me: You and a friend come across a wintry cabin where a few poor souls are ready to freeze to death. Your friend, being concerned only for himself, huddles in the corner trying to stay warm. You, on the other hand, busy yourself for the sake of those about to perish. You rub their limbs and shoulders, you chop wood to build a fire for them. In all of this, you are warmed, even more than they, while your selfish friend shivers away in his lonely corner. The application is clear.

6) *Pride.* For many of us, if we could speak to a great and famous man, we would do it. If we were the main speaker at a prestigious evangelistic event, we would brim with boldness. But to stop everything for some "nobody"? To have the day interrupted when we know full well that we will get no public recognition for our efforts? I am happy to be known by men as a "great evangelist" ... but am I happy to be unknown to any but God (and Satan) as the same?

May the Lord Jesus give us hearts that would rather be found in a smoky hovel with a dear wretch who needs Jesus than preaching in a cathedral to those the world deems important. Let us never forget how low Jesus stooped for us!

7) Finally, *ignorance of the duty, privilege, and power to tell others* keeps many of us silent. Perhaps you do not know that Jesus has commissioned *you* to seek out poor Hell-bound souls and tell them the Gospel. Perhaps we are unaware of the privilege to which we have been called! Look: the *only thing* more wonderful than going to Heaven is taking someone there with you. Perhaps we do not realize that the Holy Spirit will empower us in this work. A weak, simple saint can share Jesus as effectively as a trained theologian (maybe better!), because it is *God's Work,* not his. Remember, it was broken Naomi who was used by Israel's God to bring the Moabitess Ruth to Himself! Pray and ask God to give you ... even *you* ... the power to live out your privilege of sharing Jesus.

Finally, I want to bless you with the following motives for sharing your faith:

First, a vital and encouraging Bible passage:

May our Lord Jesus Christ himself and God our Father, who loved us and by his grace gave us eternal encouragement and good hope, encourage your hearts and strengthen you in every good deed and word. (2 Thessalonians 2:16,17)

Consider: *We are spreading the fame of Jesus.* Can there be a better motive for evangelism? People talk about what they love. People are happy when someone they love is loved by others. When we tell others about Jesus and His Gospel, His fame spreads in hearts and homes, cultures and countries. What can be more wonderful than Jesus being famous tomorrow where He is unknown today!

Consider: *What does this means to Jesus?* He gave up Heaven and gave His blood! Can we not do a little, when He has done so much?

Consider: *The state of our lost friends, brothers, sisters, neighbours is pitiful.* Most of them are sick, and do not even know it! If *we* do not care for their souls, who will? May we not be found guilty of their blood, having failed to compassionately speak to them about Jesus (see Acts 20:26). We can be sure that God will work the miracle in hearts if we will just speak to others His warnings and wonders.

Consider: *You will know unspeakable Joy* in eternity and for eternity when in Heaven you embrace those you once told about Jesus, whom the Holy Spirit then converted. To see their once ravaged faces now beautified, their once broken bodies now glorified, their abundant joy ... knowing that you had some part to play in it all!

125

You can be an instrument used by God to bring another to Jesus! Perhaps you do not have millions to give away to charity. Perhaps you cannot draw thousands to hear you preach. Maybe your public gifts are unimpressive and you are not considered much among men, even in the Church. But *Heaven* sees, and *Hell* sees, and to be famous before the throne of Grace and hated before the gates of Hell for telling a poor sinner about Jesus outweighs all other gifts and riches you might have to offer.

Consider: *What a blessing a new Christian is to the Church here on earth*. Almost nothing brings joy and revival into a company of believers like a newborn Christian. When Saul became Paul, when Lydia, the jailor, the eunuch, Lazarus, Cornelius and John Mark came to Jesus, what life came to the fledgling Church! If we will just do our duty to our neighbours in private, what life will come to the Church in public!

Consider: *What good sharing Jesus will do to us!* If we knew this, we would begin *today* and waste no more time in excuses and waiting. God multiplies grace to us when we give grace away. In His Kingdom, the more we give, the more we gain! There is nothing better for your heart than telling someone about Jesus. You might be sad: Tell someone about Jesus. You might be ill and in pain: Tell someone about Jesus. You might be struggling with sin: Tell someone about Jesus. If Jesus promises a reward to one who simply "gives a cup of cold water" (Matthew 10:42), what does He have in store for those who offer *Jesus* to the thirsty soul?

Sharing Jesus will bring joy to your heart and peace to your conscience. It will stir up love within. It will offer your friends eternity. Do not stop at the temporary discouragements. Some may despise you now, but they will love you later.

Those who are wise will shine like the brightness of the heavens, and those who lead many to righteousness, like the stars for ever and ever. (Daniel 12:3)

Scriptures to Ponder:

Come and see what the Lord has done, the desolations he has brought on the earth. ... Come and see what God has done, his awesome deeds for mankind! (Psalm 46:8; 66:5)

Then they called them in again and commanded them not to speak or teach at all in the name of Jesus. But Peter and John replied, 'Which is right in God's eyes: to listen to you, or to him? You be the judges! As for us, we cannot help speaking about what we have seen and heard.' (Acts 4:18-20)

I am a debtor both to Greeks and non-Greeks, both to the wise and the foolish. That is why I am so eager to preach the gospel also to you who are in Rome. For I am not ashamed of the gospel, because it is the power of God that brings salvation to everyone who believes: first to the Jew, then to the Gentile. For in the gospel the righteousness of God is revealed – a righteousness that is by faith from first to last, just as it is written: 'The righteous will live by faith. (Romans 1:14-18)

Questions to Consider:

1) What motivates you to share Jesus?

2) What keeps you from sharing Jesus?

3) Discuss how telling others about Jesus and His Gospel, i) spreads His fame; ii) brings joy to the miserable; iii)

brings new life to the Church; iv) brings new life to you. Which motivates you the most?

4) Do you really believe that the Holy Spirit will enable you to tell others about Jesus?

Chapter Thirteen

Motivation for a Heaven-Minded Life

We have together begun to see something of what Heaven is like. I hope your appetite is stirred! Perhaps you have now thought more about your Rest than ever before. What I want to do now is help you to apply what we have learned toward your heart, your mind, and your actions. I want to present to you the clear motivations for living a Heaven-minded life.

You have, no doubt, heard others say that Heaven-mindedness removes us from earthly usefulness. I want to challenge that! I want to propose and prove just the opposite: that Heaven-mindedness produces radically transformed living, to the glory of God and the good of all.

What follows is meant to be a challenge to you. If we were sitting together, I would be looking you straight in the eyes, and speaking with all my love and earnestness. Can there be anything more important than Heaven? What eclipses Jesus and His Gospel? If I could "require" you I would, but all I can really do is earnestly appeal to you to: (1) Take hold of your heart and rebuke it for its deliberate worldliness, leaving worldly foolishness behind. (2) Stop feeding at the troughs of this world and begin to feast *now* on Heaven's bounty, taking hold of your thoughts and turning them away from their endless obsession with trivialities. (3) Instruct your soul that it is time to get serious about eternity, learning the habit of placing your thoughts and heart *above,* where Christ is. (4) Begin now to develop new affections and habits which honour God and eternity, learning to swim in the rivers of God's pleasures instead of the mud-puddles of Satan's.

129

There will be times in your pursuit of a Heavenly life when your heart will be your own worst enemy. You will have to order it back to its post! You will have to rebuke it for its worldliness, laziness, and coldness towards God. But the effort will be worth it a thousand times over. For, when you have traveled a little way, when you have trained your heart and mind and inner self to move from the temporary to the Eternal, when your saved spirit has gotten mastery over your foolish flesh, you will find yourself nearing the very suburbs of Heaven. You will begin to see and smell and taste of a New World. You will begin to hear the songs of Heaven and the happy laughter of its inhabitants. You will discover a sweetness in God's ways and in His appointed works, seeing as never before that following Jesus is the way of true joy. More, your heart and soul will be abundantly comforted. In the midst of all the trials and groanings of this broken life, you will be discovering a continual river of refreshment of which the lazy and worldly can know nothing.

Let's remember what the Bible says to us:

Since, then, you have been raised with Christ, set your hearts on things above, where Christ is, seated at the right hand of God. Set your minds on things above, not on earthly things. For you died, and your life is now hidden with Christ in God. When Christ, who is your life, appears, then you also will appear with him in glory. (Colossians 3:1-4)

Dear ones, by the authority I have as a minister of the Gospel, as an ambassador of Jesus, I appeal to your hearts. Considering Heaven is more than just advice. Pursuing a Heavenly life is more than just an option. It is in fact the sacred duty of every child of grace. Fixing an eye on our Rest, placing our hearts and minds above with Jesus is life-transforming, God-honouring, mission-motivating. If you remember anything I have ever taught you, remember this! If I have ever been able to have any impact upon your life, may it be now and about Heaven!

When we are oriented rightly, there are inconceivable joys to be had now in considering what is to come ... joys that far outweigh any other we might know. The problem is that we are so off course, so caught up in the trivial and temporal, that we are bored with any thoughts of the meaningful and eternal. Let's bring this down to an earthly level: We do not find it hard to think about dear friends, or anything else that is dear to us. We easily think about earthly things that we treasure, even as a cold man dreams of a warm house, or a hungry man does a ready meal. The thought of, the sight of, the hope of them, is motive enough to determine our course and direction. A sailor on a stormy sea does not need to be cajoled into the harbor ... he *seeks after it.* You cannot keep him from it.

We clearly know how to be earnest and constant in all sorts of things that we can see. But my own experience, and my knowledge of yours, tells me that when it comes to the Eternal and Unseen, our hearts quickly wander and our feet quickly grow weary. We would think that the thought of being with Jesus, in a place with no sin, death, and pain, that crowns, and crystal rivers, redeemed cultures, and glorified bodies would be all the motive we need to be done with sin and foolishness. But – ah – as long as we are in these corrupt bodies and in this fallen world - all these wonderful future blessings somehow are too weak to motivate us day by day, year by year until we see Jesus. We sputter along, toying today with holiness and tomorrow with sin, rejoicing one moment and cursing the next, resting in Jesus now and suddenly striving in ourselves. So, what follows is intended to motivate you toward pursing Heaven. I am confident that if you ponder these earnestly, and

131

apply yourself to them, that they will have a good effect upon your hearts, and motivate you to follow hard after Jesus and His Heaven. Please do not just read the words. Do not let them fall to the ground like wasted seeds. Press them upon your hearts, judge yourselves by them, and determine to be as (or more!) earnest here as you already are in so many fading things.

Twelve Motives for a Heaven-Minded Life

1) A heavenward heart is *clear evidence of a true saving work in your life.* You can be sure of this: Your heart and your treasure will always be found together. God – the God who saves sinners - is in Heaven, so, if He is your treasured Saviour, your heart will already be in Heaven.

We go to Heaven in four stages: First, our *Treasure* goes there as we shift our affections from the things of earth to Jesus, who is now in Glory. Then, our *hearts* go as we place our affections where our Treasure is. Then follow our *spirits* the moment we die, and, finally, our *bodies* when they are raised in glory.

So, our hearts should be, if not fully, at least increasingly in Heaven right now. A heart set upon Heaven is a heart set upon God. It is seeking enjoyment from another place, and is increasingly free from the tangles of this world. There can be no greater evidence of saving grace in a life. Find some simple Christian whose learning is little, whose gifts are few, whose strength is waning, but whose heart is yearning for Jesus and whose thoughts are often on Heaven, and there you have a true trophy of grace. He is already living in the suburbs of God's City. I would rather be that man than the most honoured and learned man in this world. I would rather live and die with his heart than be the most gifted and regarded man in this world's terms.

Christian, you say you love God. Well, prove your words by getting your heart where He is. I assure you, get your heart in Heaven and the rest is sure to follow!

But store up for yourselves treasures in heaven, where moths and vermin do not destroy, and where thieves do not break in and steal. For where your treasure is, there your heart will be also. (Matthew 6:20,21)

2) A heavenly heart is *the noblest and best heart you can have.* The better your heart, the better your usefulness, joy, happiness, and blessing to God and others. Some Christians have comparatively worldly hearts. They scratch about like turkeys when they could soar like eagles. God has made us to have our heads held upwards toward Heaven. To cultivate a heart that is fixed above is to cultivate a healthy and happy heart. To be in the presence of a Jesus follower who has placed his heart above with Jesus is to be in the company of a rare and excellent jewel. A Christian who has learned to get his joy straight from Heaven is like a mountain that rises above the rest, or a tree that stands taller than the others.

That man or woman ... be he or she ever so simple ... who, with an open Bible and a trusting heart, visits Heaven often will have a heart more valuable and more to be desired than all the gifts and abilities this world has to offer.

> *How lovely is your dwelling-place,*
> *Lord Almighty!*
> *My soul yearns, even faints,*
> *for the courts of the Lord;*

133

my heart and my flesh cry out
for the living God ...
Blessed are those who dwell in your house;
they are ever praising you.
Blessed are those whose strength is in you,
whose hearts are set on pilgrimage.
As they pass through the Valley of Baka,
they make it a place of springs;
... They go from strength to strength,
till each appears before God in Zion.
(Psalm 84:1-7)

3) A heavenward heart is *a joyful heart.* Friends! This life is a hard life. It is a storm. If we are seeking our joy and comfort from this fallen world we are sure to end with broken hearts and sad spirits. It is unavoidable. Just ask Solomon!

I denied myself nothing my eyes desired;
I refused my heart no pleasure ...
Yet when I surveyed all that my hands had done and what I had
toiled to achieve,
everything was meaningless, a chasing after the wind;
nothing was gained under the sun ...
So I hated life.
(Ecclesiastes 2:10,11,17)

But, it is impossible to have a heart at home in Heaven and be without comfort. As fire warms, so being in the Spirit brings joy. Why are some Christians happier than others? And, why are so many Christians who are burdened with the hardest lives the happiest of all? Because they have learned to gather their joy elsewhere – directly from Jesus.

There really is a springtime for your soul. There is a time and place where the ice thaws and the shoots of life burst forth. The birds return with song and the time of rejoicing comes. Winter sadness is gone, and it is time to rise and praise our gracious God. Christian! Get your mind above. Get your heart where Jesus is. Know that right now, in God's view, you are with Him in Heaven, for He sees your glorious end from the beginning :

And God raised us up with Christ and seated us with him in the heavenly realms in Christ Jesus (Ephesians 2:6).

God gives joy as we seek it. Just as He gives a bee honey as he seeks nectar, He gives us joy as we open our Bibles, raise our hearts heavenward, and *apply ourselves* to discover the delights and wonders He has prepared for us. As long as we forage through the garbage of this world, we cannot expect to feast at the table of His delights. Just as you will thrill a worldly man if you show him gold, so God will thrill a heavenly man by showing him the treasures of His Rest. So, believe what the Bible says about Jesus, you, the Gospel, and Heaven. Learn to live in anticipation of your future joy, and joy – in increasing measure - will be yours today.

Birds feed their young as they wait passively in their nests with their mouths agape. But that is not the way God gives us His joy. Look instead to the farmer. He plows, sows, digs, weeds, and the land brings forth its bounty. So as we plow and sow and dig and weed in our hearts, God brings forth His bounty of joy.

We are as happy as we want to be.

A Christian's joy is not irrational or unexplainable. It is not just a "mood." It is solid and explainable, for it is rooted in the Gospel and fixed in Heaven. Go and get it!

If you keep my commands, you will remain in my love, just as I have kept my Father's commands and remain in his love. I have told you this so that my joy may be in you and that your joy may be complete. (John 15:10,11)

4) A heavenward heart is *a powerful weapon against temptation and sin.* Yes, God can, in His mercy, protect us supernaturally from sin and temptation. He no doubt sometimes does this. But it is presumption to ask and expect Him to do this if we are not doing what He has asked and expects us to do. He is asking and expecting us to place our hearts and minds on Him and His Heaven. He is asking and expecting us to think about "whatever is true, whatever is noble, whatever is right, whatever is pure, whatever is lovely, whatever is admirable ...excellent or praiseworthy..." (Philippians 4:8).

A vacant mind is the devil's workshop. He will work his works without hindrance in a disengaged mind. He will fill an empty space with thoughts of evil and temptations. But! When heart and mind are in Heaven with Jesus, Satan has no point of entry! Let that fiend come with any enticement toward evil and the mind busied in Heaven will answer him as Nehemiah answered his enticing enemies:

I am doing a great work ... why should the work cease, whilst I leave it, and come down to you? (Nehemiah 6:3 KJV)

This is obvious! A heart that is caught up in Jesus, a mind that is thinking great and noble thoughts, gives no space for the works of the tempter. But this takes work on our part. We must be deliberate about this. If we are letting dust gather on our Bibles, if we are not feeding good into our hearts and minds, while we lazily allow Satan to toy with us, we cannot expect anything but defeat. But be sure of this: If we fix ourselves above, where Christ is, Satan's flaming arrows cannot reach us.

When our thoughts are on Heaven, we see all things more clearly. We see sin for what it really is. We see just how deadly it is. We can get a clearer view of Hell from Heaven than we can from earth. Just as in a war campaign we set our sentinels on high places so that they can see farther, so we from the heights of Heaven can see movements of the enemy that we would otherwise miss. It is easier to snare a bird on the ground than in the air. The higher we are the safer we are. Satan's snares are laid in the low, dark places. He cannot catch a Christian who is dwelling in the higher, brighter realms.

A Jesus follower who dwells in the world above will grow in wisdom ... wisdom that will give him power over sin. When our minds are filled with God and His wisdom, when our Bibles are well-worn from sacred use and our knees are well-worn from seeking after God, we grow in a wisdom that gives us great advantage over sin. Sin flourishes where foolishness reigns. Sin retreats where wisdom reigns. Wisdom reigns when one's heart and mind are fixed above. A man or woman might be unlearned in terms of the things of this world, but he might be wiser than all the scholars in all the halls of learning.

It is not just the one who knows the most, but the one who loves the most who has the greatest power over sin. And, the one who dwells most with Jesus, who *abides* with Him, grows to love Him more than the one who does not. The more time we spend with Jesus, the more precious He becomes to us. It cannot be any other way! Do you want to drive sin out of your heart? Drive it out with a greater love. Drive it out with the love of Jesus reigning where the love of sin once held sway. You will spend time with what you love.

> *Unto you therefore which believe he is precious ...*
> (1 Peter 2:7 KJV).

Imagine trying to convince a simple man that sugar is not sweet. You can try endless, learned arguments, but you will not prevail. Why? Simply because that simple man has *tasted* the sweetness. So, once we have tasted the sweetness of God's love, and begun to feast upon the delights of Heaven, the bitterness of sin and guilt must lose their savour. A heavenward life is beginning now to experience the love of God that is beyond human knowledge (Ephesians 3:14-21). Loving what is sweet is perhaps the best way to come to hate what is sour.

> *Taste and see that the Lord is good; blessed is the one who takes refuge in him.* (Psalm 34:8)

God will especially protect the one whose heart is resting in Him. When we are abiding in His Rest, Satan has no opportunity to reach us with his flaming arrows.

Dear Christian! If you are assaulted by your enemy, if sin and temptation are hounding you, flee to Jesus! Take your thoughts and affections upwards. Get close to God. He will receive you. He is at His best when we are at our worst! He is strongest when we are weakest!

> *For you have been my refuge,*
> *a strong tower against the foe.*

> *I long to dwell in your tent for ever*
> *and take refuge in the shelter of your wings.*
> (Psalm 61:3,4)

5) A Heaven-aimed heart will *put life and energy into your duties and gifts.* Heavenly Christians are life-filled Christians. Those aimed at Heaven find themselves energized for earthly service. They do not just sit about staring at the clouds; they are busy doing what will affect eternity. Strangers to Heaven are sluggish on earth. It is our happy hope of our Rest which gives us zeal for work and perseverance when work is wearisome. It is the hope of a reward which motivates the farmer and the runner. So it is with the Jesus follower. If soldiers and sailors will risk all for victory and treasure, just imagine what life and energy will be put into your Christian journey if you grow a heavenward heart! What treasure there is for us in Heaven! Jesus Himself!

You make known to me the path of life; you will fill me with joy in your presence, with eternal pleasures at your right hand. (Psalm 16:11)

Examine your own experience. When you have been feeding on the junk food of this world, you grow lazy and fat in your race to your Rest. You know this is true. But when you have been feeding on the feast of God's grace, drawing your nourishment from the samplings of Heaven's banquet, you find your stride in the heavenly race. Why does a given brother or sister work with such zeal, speak with such grace, love with such constancy? You know why. He has been with Jesus. Here are two preachers: both are orthodox, evangelical, trained, believing. But one plods. His work is heavy but not heavenly. His sermons are correct but a chore to endure. The other walks in a world of joy. His work is weighty but heavenly. His sermons are packed with *life*. It is clear that one visits Heaven and the other does not. It is one thing to prepare a sermon, it is another thing to prepare yourself to preach that sermon. Give me a Heaven-minded preacher over a scholar any day. Give me a preacher who is both even more!

The graces, gifts, and callings in a Christian's life are sourced in Heaven with God and they must be fed and nourished from there. Without time seeking the Lord, putting your heart in Heaven, you will be like an unlit lamp and your work like an altar with the fire gone out. But go be with God, get one coal from His heavenly altar of grace, and everything changes. Make it your life's habit to go there every day, or you will become weary in your way.

Just as the moon is brightest when it fully faces the sun, so you will be brightest when you fully look upon the face of God. You can tell when a person has been spending time alone with God. I promise you, "since we have confidence to enter the Most Holy Place by the blood of Jesus, by a new and living way opened for us through the curtain, that is, his body" (Hebrews 10:19,20), that if you will do so you will find power in your words and work, such that people will say "never has anyone spoken like this...surely this man has been with Jesus." And God will be glorified (Mark 1:27; Acts 4:13).

He gives strength to the weary
and increases the power of the weak.
Even youths grow tired and weary,
and young men stumble and fall;
but those who hope in the Lord
will renew their strength.
They will soar on wings like eagles;
they will run and not grow weary,
they will walk and not be faint. (Isaiah 40:29-31)

6) Looking heavenward with the eyes of faith *brings great comfort in times of affliction.* There is not a better medicine than thinking about Heaven. Our spirits are sustained in the midst of suffering, we are encouraged to praise rather than complain, and our resolution is fortified that we will not deny Jesus in the midst of our trials. I can tell you from personal experience: Had it not been for that foretaste of Heaven, my sufferings, and my impending death, would have been far more bitter to taste.

Seeing Heaven with the eyes of faith puts suffering in perspective. No prison door can keep us from being seated with Christ in Heaven. Paul and Silas were in Heaven while they were in prison (Acts 16:25). Jesus sweetens every painful situation. He stands and speaks "Peace be with you!" in the midst of our fears and failures (John 20:21).

We need to get this: It is not the place or the circumstance that gives rest, but the presence of Christ and an apprehension of the Rest that awaits us. Martyrs have more peace than their persecutors because they see beyond the flames to the glory that awaits them. When our hearts are at rest above with Jesus, neither the times of pleasure nor the times of tribulation can own us.

There is nothing affecting you that your coming resurrection will not fix!

Friend! Learn to keep your soul above, where Christ is. Heavenly perspective helps us to see both the hard journey and the glorious end. This is the transforming power of faith in Jesus and His Gospel. We need to see not only the seed sown and dying, but the flower blooming in life. We need to see not only ourselves laboring and sweating, but being served at the

Master's table (Luke 13:29)! Wicked men may do their worst to us, our own sin may bring us sorrow, our bodies may bring us sickness and pain, and God may lead us through valleys of His design. In it all a heavenly vantage will be a tonic for our souls.

Therefore we do not lose heart. Though outwardly we are wasting away, yet inwardly we are being renewed day by day. For our light and momentary troubles are achieving for us an eternal glory that far outweighs them all. So we fix our eyes not on what is seen, but on what is unseen, since what is seen is temporary, but what is unseen is eternal. (2 Corinthians 4:16-18)

7) The Heaven-minded Christian *is the most earthly useful Christian.* Need help? Need good solid, counsel? Find a brother or sister whose heart is at rest with Jesus and whose mind is on eternity. Imagine that you are in a strange country (in reality, you are, 1 Peter 2:11). Weary and lonely, you come upon a friend from your homeland. He has recently been there! What comfort and encouragement he is able to give to you as he brings news and vision from the land you love! A heavenly Christian is a source of great comfort and joy to all fellow citizens of Heaven who cross his paths. He has been there in the spirit! He is acquainted with the things you love the most.

I can enjoy speaking with learned theologians about deep things and disputable matters. But give me a heavenly brother or sister, and my soul will be nourished in a better way. Theological acumen is prone to lead to pride. A heavenly conversation with a heavenly Christian leads to humility and richness of the soul. Right doctrine is vital, but it needs to be refreshed with the dew of Heaven if it is to bring true help and life.

Remember when the woman broke the vial of perfume over Jesus (John 12:1-3)? Remember how the fragrance filled the entire house? In the same way, a Heaven-hearted Jesus follower spreads the fragrance of Christ wherever he travels:

But thanks be to God, who always leads us ... in Christ's triumphal procession and uses us to spread the aroma of the knowledge of him everywhere. (2 Corinthians 2:14)

Whoever comes into the range of a heavenly person is influenced by the fragrance. What a blessing it is to have a minister who is not just orthodox (essential) but heavenly (equally essential!). Too many pastors stop at their doctrine and do not pursue the very fragrance of Jesus. They do not aim at Heaven. They are of little help. But a pastor, or a sister or brother, or any Christian, who travels with Jesus, abides with Jesus, visits Heaven, what life-giving help they become! An hour in their presence will do more good than a year in the presence of an earth-bound man – no matter how learned, wealthy, or powerful.

Find a Heaven-bound, Heaven-minded person and connect your heart to him or her and see how you are transformed. Watch how he forgives when wronged, is meek when others are angry, is charitable when others are self-seeking. Become such a person, and see what a help you will be to countless needy souls around you!

As far as I am concerned, I would rather walk with a heavenly man than with the worldly wise and powerful any day, and at any price.

Flee the evil desires of youth and pursue righteousness, faith, love and peace, along with those who call on the Lord out of a pure heart. (2 Timothy 2:22)

8) A Heaven-Aimed person *honours God above all.* Do you want to honour God? Put your heart and mind in Heaven. Treasure Him above all else, and your heart will be where your Treasure is. Imagine a good, loving, faithful father who provides all things abundantly for his children. Imagine that those children choose to feed on trash and to live in rags. Are they honouring their father? Did the wild boy in Jesus' story (Luke 15:11ff) honour his father? When we, who call God our Father, choose to feed on the husks of this world, ignoring the one to come, when we live mindless of what Jesus is now preparing for us (John 14:2), are we not dishonouring God with every breath?

We honour God when we live in anticipation of being with Him. We honour God when we think often about what His Son is preparing for us. We honour God when we, considering that we are now seated with Christ in Heaven, declutter our minds and ponder our destiny in Jesus.

We are the Bride of Christ! Soon our Bridegroom will appear for us. What earthly bride does not live in joyful anticipation and diligent preparation? Is it right that we live today as though we were not betrothed to the King? Is it right today that we do not live in joyful hope and earnest preparation? Should we be adulterating ourselves or purifying ourselves in light of our fast-approaching wedding day?

When a Christian places his hope and joy above, where Jesus is, he honours his God, and he is sure to be honoured by his God (1 Samuel 2:30).

9) If we ignore this duty *we flatly disobey God and lose great comfort for our souls.* God is not indifferent to this! He is not passive on this matter. He has made it a both duty and a welcome comfort for us to place our thoughts in Heaven. Thus, by this double strength rope does He draw us toward Heaven.

If you are indifferent to what God is serious about, certainly this is a grave situation. We tend to be serious about what God is little concerned with - trivial foolishness, and blasé to what God is most earnest about - Heaven and His Kingdom. He has a "to do list" for us, and ours needs to match His. On top of that list is: "Place your heart in heaven, where your treasure is." *He* knows better than we what is best for us. He knows what will comfort, guide, and guard us through this stormy life far better than we. We disobey God and bypass wonderful Bible truths when we fail to aim ourselves toward our Rest.

We frustrate the plans and promises of Jesus for us when we ignore His promises about Heaven. They are intended to orient us rightly. They are for our joy, correction, and sanctification. The saints in Glory have perfected spirits in His presence, but we have perfected promises in His Word. His promises assure us of the coming fullness. You would do better to lose your arm, your eye, your friends, your very life than to lose one of His promises for you about Heaven. God is happy to give us His Book and within it to reveal to us His plans for us, and to bring us to familiarity with His eternal love for us. He does this so that our present joy will be full, and so that we will happily forsake all for Him and His Heaven. He does this to embolden us against sin and Satan. He does this because He is excited about sharing His Heaven with us! He tells us now that we are heirs to His Kingdom, where there is no night, no death, no pain, no sorrow, no sin. Yet! We so often live as if He has told us nothing! We live enamored with sin

145

and weighed down with sorrow as though Christ had been silent about His plans for us. We would rather trust in foolish tales and stories about "the hereafter" than know what the Bible says about Heaven. It is as though the Holy Spirit might just as well not have given us the Bible!

If an earthly prince had promised you some vast estate and all the treasures this world could offer, would you not visit it often until it was fully yours? Would you not delight in the prince's promise and often be caught dreaming of your inheritance? Would you not forever be speaking well of your prince to others and ache to see him ever dishonoured? Would the certainty of his promise not motivate you to live in such a way that your princely friend was honoured and you were ready to receive your prize? Well, God, the Father, Son, Spirit has promised that all that is His is soon to be yours. Dare you not live every day in the bright light of that promise?

His divine power has given us everything we need for a godly life through our knowledge of him who called us by his own glory and goodness. Through these he has given us his very great and precious promises, so that through them you may participate in the divine nature ... (2 Peter 1:3,4)

10) We should think much about God in His Heaven *because God in His Heaven thinks much about us.* If the Lord of all the universe, who alone is from Everlasting to Everlasting, who needs nothing outside of Himself, can stoop to think about us, frail creatures of dust, should we not think about Him? More than just thinking about us, He *delights* in us. His thoughts are ever toward us:

The Lord your God is with you, the Mighty Warrior who saves. He will take great delight in you; in his love he will no longer rebuke you, but will rejoice over you with singing. (Zephaniah 3:17)

> *How precious also are thy thoughts unto me,*
> *O God! how great is the sum of them!*
> *If I should count them, they are more in number than the sand:*
> *when I awake, I am still with thee.*
> (Psalm 139:17,18 KJV)

If God took as little delight in us as we do in Him; if He forgot us the way we forget Him, we would be in a troubled state! Friend, God follows you with a faithful love every day, showering you with endless care and mercy. He is careful toward you when you are careless toward yourself and toward Him. He regards you when you forget Him, faithfully working all things to the good of your soul. He charges His angels to watch over you and sets a guard over you day and night. He loves you far more than you love Him.

And yet, can you find it in your heart – still – to forget Him for hours, days, weeks on end? Can you leave your Bible to gather dust while you amuse yourself with endless vanities? Can you forget Heaven while He has purchased it at such great cost and joyfully prepares it for you? Could Isaiah's complaint against Israel be leveled against you?

> *The ox knows its master,*
> *the donkey its owner's manger,*
> *but Israel does not know,*
> *my people do not understand.*
> (Isaiah 1:3)

Think about this: Even a wandering ox makes its way home at night. Even a dog comes when called. Can you not bring your heart home at least once a day? Oh Christian! Get yourself home to God every morning, and learn to think of Him who constantly thinks of you.

11) Our hearts and minds should be in Heaven *because Our Father is there, and through the Gospel we belong to Him.* We pray, "Our Father who is in Heaven." If our Father, who loves us, and who has redeemed us at immeasurable cost, is in Heaven, should we not often be placing our hearts there?

Strange children! We have such a loving Father preparing a home for us, and we forget Him as we play here in a foreign land. And there is His Son, Jesus, who promises us Rest with Him, who purchased that Rest with His own blood. All of the treasures of wisdom and knowledge are hidden in Him. He prepares and waits for us. Should we not be anticipating Him often, daily, many times a day, moment by moment?

And then there are those who have gone before us - children of our heavenly Father, our brothers and sisters. Remember how we wept and mourned at their deaths? If the Bible is true, they are with Jesus, part of a vast multitude (Hebrews 12:1,23). Should we not joyfully and often anticipate our reunion?

If you were a stranger in a strange land, would you not have many thoughts and hopes of home? How often would you think of your father? Could you ever forget your siblings and dear friends safe in your home country? Why are we so forgetful of Heaven? Could it be that we are too "at home," forgetting that we are actually strangers and pilgrims here (1 Peter 2:11)?

Dear ones! May we receive grace to ever remember that our Father has "given us new birth into a living hope ... into an inheritance that can never perish, spoil or fade ... kept in heaven for you." (1 Peter 1:3,4)

12) *There is nothing else that deserves our ultimate affection and highest thoughts.* What is more important than eternity? If you are neglecting your Rest, you are gambling with your soul. You cannot afford the cost of making a mistake here. You dare not grasp at shadows at the cost of the substance. Jesus said it far better:

What good will it be for someone to gain the whole world, yet forfeit their soul? Or what can anyone give in exchange for their soul? (Matthew 16:26)

Heaven is lost not just through outright rebellion, but through careless neglect as well. It is lost through expecting earth to give what only Heaven can, from time what is only available from eternity, from below what only can be found above. You do not need to learn this lesson by experimenting with your own soul! Believe what God has told you. Learn from the thousands who have already made ruin of their lives!

Of course, duty and necessity require that we busy ourselves with many mundane things: jobs, families, bodies. These things are not bad. They become bad when we expect from them what they cannot give: Rest. If your life is defined by nothing but these things, if they form your boundaries, then you are no different from the beasts of the fields. Your values are essentially pagan:

So do not worry, saying, "What shall we eat?" or "What shall we drink?" or "What shall we wear?" For the pagans run after all these things, and your heavenly Father knows that you need them. But seek first his kingdom and his righteousness, and all these things will be given to you as well. (Matthew 6:31-33)

Earthly cares bring trouble. It is in their nature to do so. But we are citizens of Heaven! We are bound by a solemn and joyful covenant with the King of another country to not get entangled in the affairs of this rebel land. The best honours this defiant world can give are nothing compared to the least which the coming world can give!

Thou hast put gladness in my heart, more than in the time that their corn and their wine increased. (Psalm 4:7 KJV)

Better is one day in your courts
than a thousand elsewhere;
I would rather be a doorkeeper in the house of my God
than dwell in the tents of the wicked.
(Psalm 84:10)

If, like a busy bee flying flower to flower, your thoughts travel the world over looking for true sweetness, they will find none except from those things that have eternal value.

So, I have given you twelve motives for seeking Heaven and a heavenly heart. I ask you, please, to read them again ... and then again. Tell me, have I not proven to you that it is your solemn and happy duty to pursue Heaven? If you say, "No, you have not," I think that you are speaking against your very conscience. I think you know that my arguments are unassailable. If you say, "Yes, you certainly have," then I must warn you that if you do not set your heart above, your own words will one day rise up and bring a charge against you. These twelve shall then be a jury to bring a conviction against you.

Be willing to pursue Heaven and the work is half done! I know that I speak with all the earnestness I can, but it is all from a heart full of love for you.

Will you pursue God and His Heaven, or will you not?

Scriptures to Ponder:

> *One thing I ask from the Lord,*
> *this only do I seek:*
> *that I may dwell in the house of the Lord*
> *all the days of my life,*
> *to gaze on the beauty of the Lord*
> *and to seek him in his temple.*
> *For in the day of trouble*
> *he will keep me safe in his dwelling;*
> *he will hide me in the shelter of his sacred tent*
> *and set me high upon a rock.*
> (Psalm 27:4,5)

Therefore, holy brothers and sisters, who share in the heavenly calling, fix your thoughts on Jesus, whom we acknowledge as our apostle and high priest. (Hebrews 3:1)

Therefore, since we are surrounded by such a great cloud of witnesses, let us throw off everything that hinders and the sin that so easily entangles. And let us run with perseverance the race marked out for us, fixing our eyes on Jesus, the pioneer and perfecter of faith. For the joy that was set before him he endured the cross, scorning its shame, and sat down at the right hand of the throne of God. Consider him who endured such opposition from sinners, so that you will not grow weary and lose heart. (Hebrews 12:1-3)

151

Questions to Consider:

1) What keeps me from pursuing Heaven? What am I loving more than Jesus?

2) Where is my Treasure? If I examine my time, my spending, my conversation, what do I learn about what I treasure the most?

3) Of the twelve motives above, which speak most loudly to me?

Chapter Fourteen

Hindrances to a Heavenly Life

Countless miss Heaven. Why? My concern here is to show you some of the pitfalls into which many have plunged. I trust that in so doing you will be careful to follow closely the marked pathway to your Rest.

1) *Many live in unconfessed, known sin.* We all have remaining sin. The question to ask yourself is: "Have I agreed with God against myself over this sin?" Are you battling your sin or cuddling your sin? Are you asking God to help you hate it as He does or are you making excuses for it?

We must declare unceasing war against our own sins! Otherwise, we will become enslaved to our passions and appetites. They will increasingly rule over us until they have us and ruin us. The deep unseen heart sins can be the deadliest ... like jagged rocks beneath the seemingly calm surface.

Pride, seeking of one's own esteem, is without question the deadliest of all heart sins. Is your mind set aflame when others are esteemed above you? Are your emotions ready to explode when you are passed over? Do have gunpowder in your heart, ready to fire off at any wry look or sharp word?

Are you deceptive with your words? Can you twist them just enough to manipulate a situation toward your own selfish ends?

Do you cherish secret lusts? Do you bring them out for special occasions? Does your wayward heart take strange solace in your wicked imaginings? If your secret life was made public for all to see, would you run for the hills?

Are you the same person in public as in private, knowing that God sees all - all the time? Or are you a hypocrite?

Are you as diligent with your soul as a banker with his books, or a gardener with her garden? Or do you think you will gain Heaven in spite of carelessness and laziness? If you are not careful with your heart, and if you are allowing the weeds of sin to grow there, you will have an impossible time trying to think about Heaven and place your heart where Jesus is.

Listen! Heaven is open! Jesus opened it! The curtain is torn! *We* make it hard by loving what cannot enter the presence of God. *God is not the problem*!

> *Surely the arm of the Lord is not too short to save,*
> *nor his ear too dull to hear.*
> *But your iniquities have separated*
> *you from your God;*
> *your sins have hidden his face from you,*
> *so that he will not hear.*
> *For your hands are stained with blood,*
> *your fingers with guilt.*
> *Your lips have spoken falsely,*
> *and your tongue mutters wicked things.*
> (Isaiah 59:1-3)

The strongest Christian cannot put his heart in Heaven if he is entertaining willful sin. Learn to repent at the first approach of sin. Do not wait for it to take root within you! Do not crawl away from it secretly hoping it might catch up. Flee it! Become a sin hater! Be tough on yourself regarding your own sins, and gentle on others regarding theirs. Every willful sin is like water poured on fire. It will entangle your feet and trip you on your way to Heaven. No wonder Jesus taught us to pray – daily – "Lead us not into temptation"!

2) *Feeding an earthly mind will starve your heavenly mind.* Jesus said it, but we keep acting as though it does not apply to us:

No one can serve two masters. Either you will hate the one and love the other, or you will be devoted to the one and despise the other. (Matthew 6:24)

It is easy to think earthly thoughts. It is easy to get caught up in what we see. It is easy to get consumed in the here and now. But faith has to do with the future and the unseen:

Now faith is the substance of things hoped for, the evidence of things not seen. (Hebrews 11:1)

You can get comfort, strength, solace from earth - or from Heaven. Yes, God often mediates His heavenly goodness through the things of this world. There is no problem with that. But Jesus tells us of a man who believed he could draw all goodness from the earth to the neglect of God and Heaven (Luke 12:13ff). His barns, banks, and bonds had won his heart. Morning and evening he thought about his possessions, sure that his security was in them. His Bible lay somewhere under the clutter of his life. He loved to have people stare at him in awe and honour him in the streets. While his believing neighbor thought of eternal things, lived in conscious thankfulness to God, and drew strength from Heaven, he thought about his worldly success and from there sought his strength. He had turned his back upon God.

While many thought him wise, God called him a fool (Luke 12:20).

155

Yes we need to think about mundane things enough to maintain life. And yes, God has given us all things for our enjoyment. And yes, God often uses the things around us as conduits of His goodness. But it is an unavoidable rule: The more delight you seek from earth, the less you will receive from Heaven. The more your mind is here, the less it is there.

The things of this earth need to be, as it were, the outer garments which we can quickly and easily shed, while the things of Heaven we need to wear close to our hearts.

3) The next hindrance is *keeping company with earthbound people.* I would not have you avoid being with the lost for the sake of their good and hope of their salvation. They need to engage with heaven-bound people if they are to hear the Gospel and be urged to turn from Hell to Heaven. Christians are not to hide in their little enclave. My concern is spending unnecessary time in the wrong company. The Bible is clear:

He that walketh with wise men shall be wise: but a companion of fools shall be destroyed. (Proverbs 13:20 KJV)

'Bad company corrupts good character.' (1 Corinthians 15:33)

It takes energy to move heavenward. A rock will sooner propel itself skyward than your heart will move heavenward on its own. You need the company of the godly if you are going to become godly. Yes, have non-Christian friends. Yes, be a winsome witness, but make your best friendships with those who are going to assist you on your way to Heaven. This is especially important in the early years of your Christian life. You don't yet have the strength and maturity to walk a long way on your own. You need the regular and constant company of other Jesus followers, especially while you are a child in Christ.

If you can spend endless hours with fools, talking all the drivel of this world, there is a great problem with your heart. Unless you are deliberate about it, it is impossible to keep a heavenly mind in worldly company. If you have not yet discovered this, it is probably because you have never tried!

Again:

Flee the evil desires of youth and pursue righteousness, faith, love and peace, along with those who call on the Lord out of a pure heart. (2 Timothy 2:22)

4) *Arguments over disputable matters* will hinder your way to Heaven. I am not saying that Truth does not matter, and I am certainly not saying that there are not times when we must contend for Truth. But there are lesser issues in which Jesus followers often get bogged down. Pride rather than love sometimes motivates our hearts. Our goal becomes to "be right" and "win" our arguments.

Such occasions actually do great harm to our spiritual well-being. We take our eyes off of Jesus and His Heaven. We are no longer thrilled by the Gospel when we are lathered up in arguments with our brothers. True Christianity is not a matter of religious opinions but a matter of a living relationship with God via the Gospel.

If we spent as much time glorying in the Gospel and Heaven as we did fussing about matters that divide us, we would be far more useful to God. Of course I would have you well trained in the things that matter and able to defend Christian Truth whenever necessary. But in the midst may we all seek to be joyful, heavenly men and women whose time and zeal and conversation are gathered up in promoting the sure things of Christ and His Gospel, not in disputable things, the understanding of which await a clearer day.

Have nothing to do with godless myths and old wives' tales; rather, train yourself to be godly ... Don't have anything to do with foolish and stupid arguments, because you know they produce quarrels. And the Lord's servant must not be quarrelsome ... (1 Timothy 4:7; 2 Timothy 2:23)

5) *A Proud heart* will hinder your way to your Rest. Be careful of a proud heart! There is an unbridgeable gulf between a proud heart and God. It was pride that cast angels from Heaven and pride that will keep men from it. A proud heart and a heavenly heart cannot exist in the same breast.

When you are getting to know God, spending time with Him in His Word and Spirit, you cannot help but humble yourself. You see your sins and abhor them. Time with God will keep you low – where you belong. Humility attracts grace. Therefore, times that abase you, seasons or troubles that remind you of your inability and weakness draw you more closely to God and His Heaven than you might imagine. The times of ease and prosperity - what we all want and pray for - can actually be very dangerous for our souls. They can be breeding grounds for deadly pride.

God dwells with the humble, now and in eternity:

For this is what the high and exalted One says – he who lives for ever, whose name is holy: 'I live in a high and holy place, but also with the one who is contrite and lowly in spirit, to revive the spirit of the lowly and to revive the heart of the contrite.' (Isaiah 57:15)

These are the ones I look on with favour: those who are humble and contrite in spirit, and who tremble at my word. (Isaiah 66:2)

A proud spirit is a contrary and arguing spirit. It is a competitive spirit which demands to have more than his neighbour and better than his brother. Do you esteem yourself and look down on others? Do you love the applause of others but feel slighted when they criticize you or prefer another over you? Do you prefer those who think highly of you, but shun those who might not have particular regard for you? Do you love to be the best and to be known by others to be so? Are you quick to quarrel with anyone who crosses you or whose opinion challenges yours? Is your heart easily inflamed? Are you easily discouraged? Do you make much of the rich ... even the godly rich ... but little of the poor? Are you unwilling to serve God in low places? Do you have to get the credit for your accomplishments? Do you love to use your gifts so that you are seen by others to be gifted? Do you hope that when you are dead and gone people will speak well of you, regret their slights of you, and finally admire you? Are you quicker to defend yourself than to confess your faults? Are you difficult to correct? Are you more ready to teach and spout your opinion than you are to be silent and learn? Would you rather rule than submit? Are you always ready to correct and censure others, but hate it when it is your turn to be censured? Do you delight to be known as a humble person? Have you reformed yourself so that others will think better of you? Are you easily offended?

If any of the above describe you, then you are the proud possessor of a proud heart. You have effectively made yourself to be a little god. You are your own idol. In this state, you cannot have your affections set upon God. You are a living contradiction and a walking civil war.

You will be like a troubled sea whenever pride is reigning in you. Humility will bring peace, but pride brings turmoil. Humility remembers God, and God remembers the humble; pride forgets God, and God stands at odds with the proud. I beg you to be very concerned for yourself at this point. Flee to Jesus! Confess your proud heart. "Humble yourselves before the Lord, and he will lift you up." (James 4:10). I am laboring this point so because pride is as deadly a poison for your soul as there can be. Dear One! Learn to be a quiet and humble soul. Embrace everything that brings you low as a gift from your Father who loves you. Pray daily for a humble spirit. Be ever watchful of the ingress of the poison of pride. You will find no rest for your soul like the rest found at the foot of the cross as you kneel repenting of your haughtiness.

6) *Laziness* will hinder your journey toward a heavenly life. We are each as holy, heavenly and happy as we want to be. Very little hinders like laziness. If cultivating a heavenly spirit could be achieved by praying through a string of beads, or following some prescribed "three steps to a heavenly life!" plan, or taking a thousand-mile pilgrimage, or joining a monastic order, or any number of outward things, then it would be an easy thing. But growing a heavenly spirit is far more difficult than mere outward duties. It is about separating our thoughts and affections from this fallen world. It is about taking ourselves by the scruff of the neck and choosing Jesus and Heaven moment by moment over all that this world has to offer ... including ourselves. It involves holding our hearts to the fire of God's love until they begin to glow with Heaven's heat.

Any of us can perform outward religious duties. But Jesus warns us with the chilling words:

> *These people honour me with their lips,*
> *but their hearts are far from me ...*
> (Matthew 15:8)

Pursuing God inwardly, at heart level, is altogether a different work. Heaven is *up*, and it is always harder to go up than down. Do not think that you will win a heavenly frame by lying about, wasting time, and playing in the puddles of this world. Sitting at the bottom of the hill, admiring the summit, will not get your heart to the top. Many of us can and do busy ourselves with no end of good things, but to stop and spend even half an hour – even five minutes – pushing your heart toward Heaven and taking your mind there is true spiritual work.

We need to get this clear: Grace is not license for laziness but power for pursuing God. In saying that we are saved by grace alone and not by works we are *not* saying that the Christian life is a life of ease. The grace saved Jesus follower enlists as a soldier and must prepare for the battlefield. The first and toughest battlefield is right in your own heart.

Many will lose the battle for their hearts simply because they are too lazy to fight.

If you agree with me that Jesus and His Heaven are the greatest of all treasures, and that to begin now to visit there is the most holy and helpful thing that you can do, then, if your heart is lazy, take ahold of it and apply the motives we explored above relentlessly to it. Do not let the greatest Treasure in all the universe lie there in front of you while you sit with your hands in your pockets. While you roll over, pull the covers over your head, and lazily fall back to sleep, the athlete is up training for his prize, and the farmer is out in his field. Should their zeal shame yours?

Gospel work is not like the impossible burdens of legalism. It is harder in that it involves our hearts, but it is easier in that Jesus enables us to do it:

Come to me, all you who are weary and burdened, and I will give you rest. Take my yoke upon you and learn from me, for I am gentle and humble in heart, and you will find rest for your souls. For my yoke is easy and my burden is light. (Matthew 11:28-29)

I tell you, apply half the time and diligence to this as you do to endless trivialities, and you will find your lazy heart falling into line and yourself in the precincts of Heaven.

7) We are hindered *by mistaking learning about Heaven with pursuing a heavenly life.* Just like gathering building materials together is not the same as building the house, so reading, studying, discussing, and preaching about Heaven are mere preparations for our Rest. They are not themselves our Rest. They are good. They are important, but too many stop there. "I have studied the matter. I can speak on it. I can pass an exam." "Knowledge puffs up while love builds up" (1 Corinthians 8:1). Mere knowledge about Heaven can actually make a person proud, but a love for Jesus, a desire to be with Him, builds up both the lover and those around him.

Pastors! I charge you to not only gather knowledge, but to spend time in the Spirit, in Heaven, where Christ is. John was not just on Patmos, but "in the Spirit" (Revelation 1:10) when he saw the things of eternity. Prepare your message, but then prepare yourself! A blind man can learn enough to talk about colours, but an artist can *glory* in those colours, and help others to do so as well. It is hard to bring fire to others that has never warmed you. Beware of the hypocrisy of preaching what you have never experienced as though you had. Preachers might be in greater danger of missing a heavenly heart than others. We can study and speak endlessly of God's ways and thereby fool ourselves into thinking we are genuinely acquainted with them when we are not. Refresh yourself with the Water of Life and nourish yourself with the Bread of Life before you minister to others.

Scriptures to Ponder:

Finally, brothers and sisters, whatever is true, whatever is noble, whatever is right, whatever is pure, whatever is lovely, whatever is admirable – if anything is excellent or praiseworthy – think about such things. Whatever you have learned or received or heard from me, or seen in me – put it into practice. And the God of peace will be with you. (Philippians 4:8,9)

*The highway of the upright avoids evil;
those who guard their ways preserve their lives.
Pride goes before destruction,
a haughty spirit before a fall.
Better to be lowly in spirit along with the oppressed
than to share plunder with the proud.*
(Proverbs 16:17-19)

A sluggard's appetite is never filled, but the desires of the diligent are fully satisfied...As a door turns on its hinges, so a sluggard turns on his bed...A sluggard buries his hand in the dish; he is too lazy to bring it back to his mouth. (Proverbs 13:4; 26:14,15)

Questions to Consider:

1) Which hindrances most threaten your journey heavenward?
2) How do the facts of a willing God and an open Heaven motivate you to overcome whatever hinders you on your way?

3) What practical steps will you put into place to remove your hindrances and pursue a heavenly heart and life?

Chapter Fifteen

Helping You Live a Heavenward Life

We have discovered some of the wonders of what God has in store for us. The following will, if deliberately applied, help you to prepare today for the tomorrow God is preparing for you.

1) *Agree that Jesus - and His Heaven – is the only True Treasure.* The sooner you can be convinced of the inability of everything else – even the good things with which God has blessed you – to bring you true happiness, the better. If you do not truly believe that God has made you for Himself, and Heaven for you and you for Heaven, then you will not pursue it. Trials will stop your progress and this world's pleasures will carry your heart away. If, in your judgment, both temporal pain and temporal pleasure carry more value than what God has for you, then it will be impossible to place your heart in Heaven.

Overvaluing earthly things and undervaluing heavenly things will cause you to lose sight of Heaven. You will not have the resolve to fight sin. You will place an unbearable burden upon earthly things, which were not created to be supremely treasured. You will become an idolater, which will inevitably lead to brokenness.

It is not enough that something is excellent. You must *know* it to be. If you mistake gold for gravel, your desires will not be moved to it. So, in order to prioritize the pursuit of Heaven we must see that being with Jesus is more to be desired than anything else, or we will not run after it.

165

2) *Do not rest until God's Rest is truly supreme in your heart.*
Remember, the Gospel of Grace does not rock you to sleep but
awakens you to Life. We love complacency. We will naturally
seek the easiest path. And, it is easy to have a worldly heart. It
is easy to sleep. But it takes spiritual work to cultivate a
heavenly heart. It is one thing to say, "Heaven is better than
anything here below." It is another thing to apply that fact to
your heart until you believe it at heart level and live like it.

Bring your heart, bring your whole life, under scrutiny.
Examine yourself. "Am I relying thoroughly upon the Gospel
and God's Grace alone?" "And in so doing, do I know that I
have a home in Heaven, where Jesus is?" "And do I truly
believe that I will never be fully happy until I am there with
Him?" "And do I therefore know that I cannot be happy here
until I learn to place my thoughts and affections above, where
Jesus is?" "Am I living *now* in light of *then*?"

I urge you to be very diligent here. Interrogate yourself *now*,
and do not lazily wait for God's questions on Judgment Day.
"Examine yourselves to see whether you are in the faith; test
yourselves. Do you not realise that Christ Jesus is in you –
unless, of course, you fail the test? (2 Corinthians 13:5)." If you
need faithful friends or your pastor to help you here, go to
them. Be most earnest over this ... as earnest as you would be
if you were needing to make certain your body was healthy
and disease-free.

Assume nothing. Ensure all things.

Do not rest until you know that Christ is yours, you are His,
your happiness is in Heaven, and your own a title to your Rest.

3) Consider often *how close Heaven is and how soon you will be
there.* It is not far off! You might be anticipating a great day,

perhaps a family gathering or festival. But if it is still a long way off, your will rarely think about it and seldom prepare for it. But if it is next week, or tomorrow, it will be on your mind and in your preparations moment by moment. Heaven is near! Life is brief and is flying by. Death and judgment, Heaven and Hell are but a heartbeat away from each one of us. If a plague is a world away, you seldom think of it. But if it is a town away, you think of it more. But next door! You will not get it out of your mind. How foolish we are! We think death and judgment are far off. We entertain sin and worldliness and foolishness as though we had a lifetime to get serious with our souls. What did Jesus say to the careless farmer? "You fool! This very night your life will be demanded from you!" (Luke 20:20) He had no idea that morning how close eternity was. But he should have!

If we think death is far off, we might live carelessly. But when we realize that it is standing at the door – right now – we begin to think rightly. In a moment, *your life* will be just a memory to a few loved ones, then, soon, it will be just an old tale. The sum total of all your belongings and achievements –which you now treasure so - will be reduced to a shoebox in some descendant's closet.

The more often you consider this, the more you will be helped on your way to Heaven.

4) *Speaking with, and spending time with, other heavenly minded Christians* will help you on your journey. How easily do we spend their hours talking about the world! No one has to encourage us toward trivial conversation about temporal things. We do so naturally and can do so for hours on end. Yet how hard it can be to get Christians to talk about Heaven! We can talk about useless disputes, worldly foolishness, church

politics with ease. But - try to find a word about Heaven among *Christians*, let alone unbelievers!

If you want to have your heart revived, and your way to Heaven helped, find a brother or sister, or a few, who want to go to be with Jesus like you do, and *talk* with them about being with Jesus. Make it a part of your conversation. Learn this. Make it habitual. Learn to be a bearer of good news. Learn to build up others by speaking often of eternity just as you always have of sports, or money, or famous people. Spend private time with Jesus and your Bible filling your heart and mind with things that matter, and then speak of those things with others of like mind. ... Start with your wife or husband and your children around the table. If a father in Israel was to be so full of the wonders of the Law that he talked "about them when ... at home and ... along the road, when [lying] down and when [getting] up." (Deuteronomy 6:6), how much more so should we be full with the wonders of the Gospel until our hearts and mouths are overflowing!

5) Learn to use *every spiritual event to move your heart toward Heaven.* Don't waste God-given opportunities to move your heart heavenward! Surely God's purpose in communion, worship, Bible reading, prayers, sermons, Christian gatherings, is not just to busy us with "duties." These things are given to us by God to move our stubborn hearts toward our Rest.

But we must be deliberate here! And, if we can learn to make it a holy habit to always be thinking: "I need to use this time to point me heavenward," our souls will be habitually helped and made rich. Think about this with me: You receive a letter from a friend, someone far away, seldom seen, but dearly loved. How that letter can move your heart toward them! Distance is erased by words on a page. If a letter can do that, should not bread and wine, or hymns, or a warm sermon, or a quiet time with an open Bible, or warm fellowship with others be able to move our hearts toward God and bring Heaven near? Make it your aim when you read your Bible or go to a gathering to pray, or take communion, or sing a hymn, or hear a sermon to *move toward Heaven.* Be determined that you will leave that meeting with your heart in Heaven. Intend to meet with God, not just to "do a religious duty," and see what God does. Look for Jesus to brighten your heart and sweeten you with a foretaste of Heaven's delights at every opportunity.

Don't waste God-given grace-events. Realize that you are desperate for God. Be done with mere formality and custom. Stop yawning your way through worship times. Get earnest about meeting with God and getting your heart in Heaven with any and every help that God gives you!

> *As the deer pants for streams of water,*
> *so my soul pants for you, my God.*
> *My soul thirsts for God, for the living God.*
> *When can I go and meet with God?*
> (Psalm 42:1,2)

6) Likewise learn to use *every earthly event in your life to move your heart heavenward.* There is not a single event or situation which God cannot use to point your heart to Heaven if you will let Him. Just as every road has a destination, and signs which point us toward it, so God has a destination for us, and we need to see every occurrence of life as a signpost toward Jesus and His Heaven.

For instance, every joyful thing: every embrace, meal, friendship, sunny day, joyful gathering is meant to point us beyond itself and to a day when such earthly joys will be magnified forever in the presence of Jesus. If our joy stops at

169

the present blessing, we do not get the full benefit of it. Blessings are meant to enhance our joy not just in the moment, but because they promise a yet greater blessing. Imagine that someone gives you ten dollars in earnest of ten thousand he promises to give you. You will rejoice in the ten because it foretells a coming fortune. Your present joy will go beyond the ten in sure hope of the ten thousand. If your rejoicing stops with the ten, you lose the full benefit of the ten. Your joy is diminished, and your praise of your friend is as well. You might praise your friend for the ten, but you are not praising him for the ten thousand, even though it is just as surely yours. To praise him in the gift of the small thing for the certainty of the great thing speaks of your confidence in his faithfulness. Teach yourself to use every daily blessing to move your heart and mind heavenward. In so doing your joy will be enriched beyond the momentary pleasure and God's worth and faithfulness will be magnified in your praise.

Likewise, instead of complaining about hardships, as though God were not all wise and all good toward you, learn to use them to press you further up the road to your Rest. Let God use them to wean you from your love of ease and creature-comfort. During the bad times, stir your spirit to praise Jesus for a day when there will be no more pain or sorrow. Know that this hardship is doing a good work in you to humble you, correct your wayward ramblings, and make you yearn for Heaven. It is not without its purpose, unless through a bitter, unbelieving spirit you let it be.

When the Lord assures us that "in all things God works for the good of those who love him, who have been called according to his purpose." (Romans 8:28), what greater "good" can be spoken of other than preparing us for eternity with Him? So learn to see all things – pleasant and painful, small and great - as designed by your loving God to direct you heavenward.

7) *Spend much time praising Jesus for all His grace and goodness.* Heaven's citizens praise God. It is their happy business. We can join in that business now, and in so doing, our hearts will be raised heavenward. When you lift your heart and voice in praise, you are joining with the angels. You can do nothing higher as a redeemed person. Learn to praise God in and for everything. Learn to join with the saints in Glory. Begin to do now what you will do in the very presence of Jesus forever.

> *I will give thanks to you, Lord, with all my heart;*
> *I will tell of all your wonderful deeds.*
> *I will be glad and rejoice in you;*
> *I will sing the praises of your name, O Most High.*
> (Psalm 9:1,2)

How easy it is to nurture a bitter, complaining spirit! It takes no effort to become a morose, earthbound creature of dust. But to live as one who is created and redeemed to inhabit eternity and live forever to the praise of our wonderful God requires deliberate intention. If you find it hard to nurture a praising spirit on your own, then get yourself in the presence of God's people when they gather to praise God. What can be more heavenly than to be in the company of the Heaven-bound when they are lifting their hearts and voices together toward their God above?

> *I will give you thanks in the great assembly;*
> *among the throngs I will praise you.*
> (Psalm 35:17,18)

Learn to salt your prayers with praise. Praise will lift them to the Throne of Grace. When your body is weak and your voice is silent, learn to praise with your heart. When your body is strong and your voice is able, lift heart and voice together to Heaven. When everything is dull, and it is easier to complain than to praise, don't allow yourself the luxury of self-indulgent sadness. You are a redeemed soul! Your eternity is secure! You are seated with Christ in Heaven! There is nothing happening to you right now that the Resurrection will not one day fix! Get on with the heavenly business of praise!

> *Why, my soul, are you downcast?*
> *Why so disturbed within me?*
> *Put your hope in God,*
> *for I will yet praise him,*
> *my Saviour and my God.*
> (Psalm 42:5)

8) *Rejoice always in God's love for you.* It seems obvious, but it is not. There might be nothing better for your soul than the quiet and constant consideration of God's love for you. Love has its own gravity. It has the power to draw things to it. So, if there is God in Heaven who extravagantly loves me, and I know this and dwell upon it, my heart will be drawn toward Him.

To doubt God's love for you is to kill your hopes of a heavenly heart! Why want to be in a place where you are not loved? But God has proven His love for you! It is beyond any shadow of a doubt!

God demonstrates his own love for us in this: while we were still sinners, Christ died for us. (Romans 5:8)

And, His love for us is the love of an extravagant father:

> *The Lord your God is with you...*
> *He will take great delight in you,*
> *[He] will rejoice over you with singing.* (Zephaniah 3:17)

172

And that of a warm-hearted husband:

> *I belong to my beloved,*
> *and his desire is for me.*
> (Song of Solomon 7:10)

Open your Bible and get a deeper and truer knowledge of the love of God for you, and you will soon see that your heart is moving toward Heaven, where your loving God awaits you.

9) If you will have a heavenward heart, *learn to hear and obey every prompting of God's Holy Spirit.* God leads and guides us not just by His Word, not just by providential occurrences, but by the inner promptings of His Holy Spirit. A sure way to help you on your way to Heaven is to learn to hear and obey God's Spirit. This means opening your heart to Him and asking Him to speak to your heart. When He urges you to get away from the noise of life and pray, do it. When He convicts you that some action or attitude is sinful, don't do it. When He is prompting you to reach out to a neighbour, forgive a brother, or serve an enemy, do not hesitate to obey.

Heaven will be a strange place to the soul that is stubborn, deaf, and disobedient to God's Spirit. God says:

> *I will instruct you and teach you in the way you should go;*
> *I will counsel you with my loving eye on you.*

Therefore:

> *Do not be like the horse or the mule,*
> *which have no understanding*
> (Psalm 32:8,9)

It is simple: Resist the Holy Spirit, hinder your way, obey the Holy Spirit, help your way. If you will open your heart to the Lord, He will begin to speak, guide, and prompt, always in accord with His Word. If you learn to hear and obey, you will find a heavenly heart growing within you, and you will be helped on your way to your Rest.

10)   Finally, *take care of your earthly body.*   You cannot separate your body from your soul. We are not spiritless animals, nor are we disembodied spirits. We are spiritual and physical beings. Obviously, we do ourselves great harm in neglecting our spiritual selves. The great majority of our race does just that, living like mere animals. But likewise, God made us to inhabit bodies, and they are to be cared for, governed, and cherished. They are neither to be the masters of our spirits, nor to be despised and abused.

A weary, neglected, battered body will hinder your spirit and thereby your heavenly journey. Likewise, a worshipped and pampered body will do the same. We need balance here. Our spirit is to master our body, but also to cherish it. The body is purposed to serve us and the cause of Christ. It is neither to be ignored nor indulged. It is good, but it is not god! It is not evil, as some Greeks would teach, nor worthy of all indulgence as Epicureans would teach. If the ascetic errs in abusing it and not seeing the blessing of his body, the pleasure seeker errs in being enslaved to it.

Our bodies can be like a sharp knife, or a ready tool for God to use – not rubbish to be discarded nor a gem to be pampered. Your way to Heaven will be best served by a healthy body that submits to your spirit and exists to carry the Gospel.

The body... is meant for the Lord, and the Lord for the body ...
Therefore honour God with your bodies. (I Corinthians 6:13; 20)

174

Scriptures to Ponder:

*May those who delight in my vindication
shout for joy and gladness;
may they always say, 'The Lord be exalted,
who delights in the well-being of his servant.'
My tongue will proclaim your righteousness,
your praises all day long.*
(Psalm 35:27,28)

*I have seen you in the sanctuary
and beheld your power and your glory.
Because your love is better than life,
my lips will glorify you.
I will praise you as long as I live,
and in your name I will lift up my hands.*
(Psalm 63:2-4)

*The life of mortals is like grass,
they flourish like a flower of the field;
the wind blows over it and it is gone,
and its place remembers it no more.
But from everlasting to everlasting
the Lord's love is with those who fear him,
and his righteousness with their children's children –*
(Psalm 103:15-17)

Questions to Consider:

1) How often do you think about the brevity of your life? How is it helpful to nurturing a heavenly heart?

2) Are you convinced of God's Father-heart for you? Do you believe that He wants to spend eternity with you?

3) Have you found the balance between abusing and pampering your earthly body to the hurt of your spirit?

4) Which of the above helps might be most pertinent to you?

Chapter Sixteen

Meditating on Heaven

Perhaps you are already recoiling at the word "meditation." It conjures up images of strange people engaged in even stranger practices. We think of sitting cross-legged on a cushion, emptying our minds of all thought, and gazing either into space or into ourselves.

Forget all of that.

I mean nothing of the sort when I speak of meditation!

We are not talking about trances and eerie states of consciousness. I am here speaking of the art of getting truth from your head to your heart, from the intellect to the affections. When I speak of "visiting Heaven," I mean nothing spooky. I am not talking about some out-of-the-body experience. Bibles will be open and brains lucid. The goal is not just a head full of knowledge about Heaven, but a heart full of affection. The aim is that our souls move from poverty to richness, from starvation to nourishment.

We moderns are not very good at being still. We gulp our food, hardly chewing, and rarely savouring. We are not used to thinking things through. We do not often go deep, for it is easier to stay shallow. Much of our lives are lived this way, and, when transferred to our spiritual lives, it means that we are poorly nourished even if forever busy with our religious activities. We might listen to endless sermons, but we rarely if ever *meditate* upon what we have heard. We forget them almost as soon as the day is over. We might "do our devotions," but only to rush away as soon as possible. We gulp our Bible reading just as surely as we do our food.

When was the last time you *thought* about spiritual truths until they began to warm your heart? When was the last time you thought about Heaven for more than a passing moment? Imagine that you were on the receiving end of a dream holiday to some paradise ... all paid for by a gracious friend. If it was a year away, you would think of it occasionally. Your fond anticipations would excite your heart. If it were a month away, you would think of it often ... with increasing anticipation. You would be telling your friends about it! A day away... it would occupy all your thoughts. Your heart would be warm and filled with joyful expectation. (You would also be full of praise for your gracious friend!) Well, Heaven is *near*. Very soon we will be with Jesus. Our purchased Rest is closer than we think. It should increasingly occupy our thoughts and words. We should be speaking more and more about our lavish friend, Jesus. Our hearts should be growing warmer and warmer.

Meditation is the soul-art of taking truth about Heaven and moving it from our minds to our hearts, from our thoughts to our feelings. It honours God as it appreciates and anticipates what He has purchased and planned for us. It strengthens our inner selves and in so doing empowers us to live this present life effectively for Jesus.

Meditation is transformational and indispensable.

But it is a skill to be acquired and an ability to be honed. It is an art. It is a work that engages both mind and heart. It requires *time*, but it is time well spent. It pays dividends for now and for eternity. A contemplative Christian is a rare jewel in today's Church. A contemplative Christian is a useful tool in today's world.

God made our hearts to be moved by our minds. And He made our spirits to respond to truth, even as eyes do to light or ears to sound. Now, there is a sense in which you already know how to meditate, and in fact do it all the time. Think of friends and loved ones. You consider things that are true about them: their features, characteristics, attributes. You mind dwells upon them, and soon your heart is engaged and warmed toward them. Your attitude toward them changes. You begin to long for them and consider how you hope to bless them. This is meditation and its fruit. People meditate at this level upon all kinds of things, good and bad: hobbies, sports, jobs, lust, greed, revenge. We engage our affections all the time by thinking about things until our hearts are moved. This proves that our affections work – they are not broken.

But when it comes to our spirits, because we are carnal and earthbound, we have a hard time getting our otherwise able hearts moved. We are not used to engaging our hearts over spiritual things. No wonder the Psalmist prayed so often for his heart!

> *Create in me a pure heart, O God,*
> *and renew a steadfast spirit within me.*
> (Psalm 51:10)

> *Teach me your way, Lord, that I may rely on your faithfulness;*
> *give me an undivided heart, that I may fear your name.*
> (Psalm 86:11)

Take courage. God has given us special help here. His Holy Spirit is ready to warm our cold hearts. We need to see the necessity of heavenly meditation and begin to cultivate it as a holy habit. We can have a whole head full of truth about Heaven (and we need truth about Heaven), but unless that truth is chewed upon until it is digested and becomes a part of us it will not move us and empower us. We need to progress from facts to devotion. Meditation is learning to take our thoughts and then our hearts from earth to Heaven, from passing kingdoms to the Lasting Kingdom, from time to eternity. God is ready to help us.

God is not asking us to part with meditating upon other good things. But won't you agree with me that it is past time that we begin to meditate upon the *best* thing? Trust me, nothing will make you happier, holier, and more useful than learning to bring your heart under the influence of the Truth about Jesus and His Heaven.

> *I keep my eyes always on the Lord.*
> *With him at my right hand, I shall not be shaken.*
> *Therefore my heart is glad and my tongue rejoices;*
> *my body also will rest secure,*
> *because you will not abandon me to the realm of the dead,*
> *nor will you let your faithful one see decay.*
> (Psalm 16:8-10)

I want now to help you develop your ability to meditate upon Heaven. In so doing, I first want to present three helps to you: (1) The best *times* and *seasons*, (2) the best *place*, and (3) the best *frame of spirit.*

1) The best *times and seasons.* We all know that it is good to have a regular time to meet with God in prayer and Bible reading. I want to urge you to not only do this, but to add to it the glorious practice of meditating upon Heaven. Workmen are disciplined, as are athletes. Accomplished musicians are as well. I can tell you now that if you leave spiritual work to chance, or worse, to "when you feel like it," you will most likely rarely if ever get to it. People who argue against discipline in

their spiritual lives (in the name of "sincerity" or "genuineness") end up careless and undisciplined. It is not legalistic to set a time to seek God and to deliberately put your heart where He is. It is no different from a husband and wife setting regular times to meet together or a student meeting regularly with his tutor. It does not mean you cannot do so at other spontaneous times. In fact, the spontaneous times will grow out of the deliberate times and be enhanced by them.

I cannot tell you what time will work best for you. Early mornings, before the sun rises and the day gets busy, work best for many. Jesus and the Psalmist both seemed to rise early and meet with their Father in Heaven (Mark 1:35; Psalm 57:8). Your circumstances will determine the best time for you. My counsel is that you preserve your *best* time of day for this because it is the most important thing you can do. It has benefit for time and eternity. Do not give heavenly meditation the off-cuts of your time, but the best of it.

Likewise, I cannot tell you how much time to take. That is between you and God. We are all tempered differently, and some can put their minds to a given task for hours; others cannot. What I do say - again - is that we need to grow in the holy habit of spending time with God, and it is my hope that even if you begin small ... even just a few minutes ... you will soon grow in your desire and ability to be still and be with the Lord. Agree with me that though the art of stillness is all but lost, we need to recover it to the good of our souls and the honour of God.

If you are not learning to visit Heaven regularly and often, you will be a stranger to the wonderful things of God. It is presumptuous for us to imagine that at death we will suddenly become lovers of God and His Heaven when in this life we have

181

shown so little regard for them. Certainly, evidence of being a new person in Jesus is at least some desire – growing through time – to be with Him. No tradesman hones his skill by laziness and little use of his tools. Likewise, your heart will go back to weeds in no time if not cared for and nurtured. As an untamed colt reverts to the wild if not trained, so our hearts will go backwards in no time if they are not brought regularly to Heaven. Your heart might be warmed by the fire of God today, but that does not mean it will not grow cold tomorrow if you turn to the cold.

Learn to make good use of the Lord's Day. I know that many despise, mock, or ignore it, but in it God has given us a gracious gift for the good of our souls. A day set aside to rest from our labours, which remembers the Lord's rest from His labours, is certainly a day for us to remember our coming Rest. Can there be a better day for us to visit Heaven than the day on which our Lord Jesus ascended there? Seek, like the Apostle John, to be "in the Spirit" on the Lord's Day (Revelation 1:10). Many hurt their souls by disregarding this day when they could be enriching themselves. Use your Sabbaths as steps to aid you on your way to Glory until at last you arrive there!

Next, take good advantage of the pleasant seasons, the times of spiritual refreshment and revival, to draw your heart to Heaven. How wonderful are those times when God seems so near! Those times when we seem to stand upon the mountain tops are times when our souls should take the short flight to Heaven. It is a spiritual skill to learn to discern the special seasons of grace when the wind of God's Spirit is moving toward your heavenly home. Hoist your sails of faith in those times. Do not waste them moored in the harbour of fear, familiarity, and laziness. Take such a good season as sent from Heaven itself, and cooperate with God's Spirit in moving your heart toward Heaven.

What about troubling times? They too can be redeemed and used to bring you heavenward. Instead of complaining, accusing, and languishing in unbelief, we need to use such times to wean us from the love of this world. There is scarcely a better season to walk in the courts of Heaven than when this earth is offering no comfort or joy. Don't waste hard times! Believe that God can use them for your good and His glory (Romans 8:28). Consecrate your worst days and seasons to Jesus and allow Him to draw you toward Himself and your prepared and purchased Rest.

Finally, what better time is there to meditate upon Heaven than when death is near and the messengers of God are coming to take you? Certainly, the best time to strengthen yourself with thoughts of the next life is when this life is almost ended. It is actually possible for your closing days to be your sweetest! If you are on a long and dangerous journey, does not your heart warm as home comes into view? The closer you are to your desired haven the more you think about it and rejoice in it. It is a season of special grace to be dying and drawing yourself close to Jesus and His Heaven. Do not waste it.

My soul thirsts for God, for the
living God. When can I go and meet with God?
(Psalm 42:2)

Therefore, with minds that are alert and fully sober, set your
hope on the grace to be brought to you when Jesus Christ is
revealed at his coming.
(1 Peter 1:13)

2) The best *Place.* Of course we can learn to meditate upon Heaven in each and every place and situation ... and we should learn to do so. God is equally everywhere and can therefore be

found everywhere by faithful souls. But this is not to suggest that there are not places which the serious seeker after Jesus and Heaven will not find more helpful.   Just look at the life of Jesus: Many times He found quiet places to pray and be alone with His Father (Mark 1:35; John 18:2). Likewise, He urged us to pray in secret:

But when you pray, go into your room, close the door and pray to your Father, who is unseen. Then your Father, who sees what is done in secret, will reward you. (Matthew 5:6)

In prayer as well as in heavenly meditation, it is important that we find a private place to draw near to our Father. It is my strongest advice that you make it a habit to have regular times when you withdraw from the company of others, even Christians, and find a private place from which to visit Heaven. Students have study rooms, musicians have practice rooms, authors have their private desks, artists have their studios, should not the Heaven-bound have their special place to approach God?

I am not advising that we become hermits! But I am advising that, like Jesus, we have places of solitude where we get away from the busyness of life. True, we can commune with God in a crowded place, for our spirits are always free to do so. But it is in secret that we learn the deepest things of God and Heaven. If you would do well in public with men, spend much time in private with God!

In the Bible, we seldom read of God or angels appearing to prophets in a crowd, but when they are alone. You decide: indoors or out, walking or sitting. I cannot tell you. But what I can say is, be as earnest in discovering this as a student with his studies or a musician with her instrument: "Where is the best place for me to meet with God and meditate upon His

Heaven?" Even as Jesus had Gethsemane, let your children or friends know that you have a special place, perhaps a corner of the house, a chair, a grove of trees, where you can be found alone with your God. From that place may the rivers of Heaven fill your heart every day!

3) The best *frame of spirit.* Your walk with God and your preparation for Heaven are not minor aspects of your life. They are your most important pursuits. They are worthy of your best time, your most precious place, and of the diligent preparation for your heart or spirit. Has not Jesus spent enough time in the stable and manger of your heart while lesser things have occupied the finer rooms?

It is vital that we rid our hearts, through confession and repentance, of any and everything that might grieve God and hinder our visit to Heaven. God *wants* to open His heart to us. He is not unwilling or difficult. But precious fellowship with Him needs a willingness on our part to let His Holy Spirit convict us of sinful attitudes and actions so that we can repent and ready our spirits to spend meaningful time with Him.

> *If I had cherished sin in my heart,*
> *the Lord would not have listened ...*
> *If we confess our sins, he is faithful and just and will forgive us*
> *our sins and purify us from all unrighteousness.*
> (Psalm 66:18; 1 John 1:9)

It was sin which first drove distance between God and Adam, and it is sin which does so today. But God is ready and willing and the blood of His Son speaks a constant word of pardon for us. A willingness to call sin for what it is and trust in the blood of Jesus for cleansing will keep our spirits in a place of readiness and openness to meet with God:

185

But if we walk in the light, as he is in the light, we have fellowship with one another, and the blood of Jesus, his Son, purifies us from all sin. (1 John 1:7)

But not just sin, but worldly cares will prevent you from meditating upon your Eternal Rest. How many things can occupy our hearts and cloud the light of Heaven! Look upon this as serious work. A surgeon must give all focus to his patient, an artist to a creation, a mathematician to figures. Just so, Christians should put all else away and give their best energy to meeting with God and visiting Heaven. You will face a horde of opposition when you try to get alone with God. Every temporal care and temptation will pound upon your soul. Your mind will run to and fro. But Jesus is ready to help! He invites you to give all your cares to Him so that you can meet with Him. What a Saviour!

Cast all your anxiety on him because he cares for you.
(1 Peter 5:7)

I want to impress upon you the seriousness of this work. It really is the greatest soul work. To learn while in this life to contemplate the next is perhaps the most important thing you can do. There is no drudgery in it, but there is seriousness. We are used to being earnest about all sorts of lesser matters, but we ignore this, or at best trifle at it. Be convinced that there is no person of such great earthly good like the person who regularly contemplates Heaven. Do not be content with excuses: "I am more of a Martha than a Mary" (see Luke 10:40). "I am a person of action not of contemplation." You might well be, but you still have the joyful and solemn duty to acquaint yourself with Heaven before you get there. We can begin to taste Glory while still on earth, and to have no desire to do so is strange and concerning.

If you will live joyfully, and die well, then get after this with the same zeal that you have already exhibited in endless lesser pursuits. You will find that other joys were mere child's play and fools' laughter compared to the joy of a few minutes spent in the vestibule of Heaven. To get your heart free from sin and cares so that it can be about its greatest business is a matter of first importance.

Above all else, guard your heart,
for everything you do flows from it.
(Proverbs 4:23)

Scriptures to Ponder:

Within your temple, O God,
we meditate on your unfailing love.
(Psalm 48:9)

I will sing to the Lord all my life;
I will sing praise to my God as long as I live.
May my meditation be pleasing to him,
as I rejoice in the Lord.
(Psalm 104:33,34)

One thing I ask from the Lord, this only do I seek: that I may
dwell in the house of the Lord all the days of my life, to gaze on
the beauty of the Lord and to seek him in his temple.
(Psalm 27:4)

Very early in the morning, while it was still dark, Jesus got up,
left the house and went off to a solitary place, where he prayed.
(Mark 1:35)

Questions to Consider:

1) Think about areas of your life where you have already learned to meditate. What can they teach you about how to meditate upon Jesus and Heaven?

2) What time of day/place do you think will be most helpful?

3) What will be the biggest challenge in preparing your heart to visit Heaven?

Chapter Seventeen

Helps for Meditating on Heaven

Moving from head to heart is the main work in cultivating a heavenly attitude. You will probably find that you are prone to not even think about Heaven over the course of an entire day. Having true and heartwarming thoughts about Heaven for fifteen minutes would be a major victory for many of us!

Again, we begin with Truth. Meditating on fantasy or error may get your heart somewhere, but not to Heaven. But we are not wanting to just leave Truth in the mind. We want to taste the sweetness, not just read of it. The Bible invites us to experience the Lord and His goodness:

> *Taste and see that the Lord is good.*
> (Psalm 34:8)

So, I offer what follows as help for you in your desire to place your mind and your heart on things above, where Jesus is (Colossians 3:1,2).

1) Learn to *use what the Bible gives you.* God has given us an abundance of help in His Word! He knows how hard it is to embrace things by faith when we are used to sight. Our senses are perfectly suited for this world, but we have to use our imperfect faith to see the next. It is easy to smell and see, hear and feel. This is natural. But to exercise the supernatural is altogether another matter.

It is not easy to rejoice in what we cannot see or embrace with our senses.

But it would be wrong to see our senses as the enemy of faith. Why not rather enlist them in the service of your spirit? Just as they can be a snare that keeps us from thinking spiritually, they can be a gift to help us think spiritually. They are actually intended by God to be useful to our souls, not a hindrance to them.

Have you noticed that in the Bible the Holy Spirit speaks of heavenly wonders in earthly ways? It seems that God is bringing the unseen to the world of sight and sense ... for our benefit. God presents the unimaginable to us with images that are all about us and with which we are completely familiar. For instance, Heaven is described as a city with streets of gold, with gates of pearl, and a throne in its middle. We are told that we will eat and drink at a festive table with Jesus in His Kingdom, where Jesus will share wine with us. We will shine like the sun in the sky in the presence of our Father. These are very "earthy" images, but they are given to help us think heavenly thoughts.

What is God doing here for us? Are we to take these images literally? God is conveying unimaginable things in ways that we can grasp. He is bringing Infinite Beauty to our finite abilities. He is condescending to our level, so that we can aspire to His. If He spoke of Heaven as it really is, He would speak beyond our current ability to understand, for:

Eye hath not seen, nor ear heard, neither have entered into the heart of man, the things which God hath prepared for them that love him. (1 Corinthians 2:9 KJV)

God brings Heaven within range with these vivid pictures. While it would be wrong to believe that Heaven is but the best of earth (gold, pearls, wine, rivers) it would likewise be wrong to be so "super-spiritual" that we cannot use these same things to help us take our thinking from earthly beauty to heavenly.

Think for a minute of the elaborate description of Israel's temple in the Old Testament. Page after page, chapter upon chapter describing an earthly tabernacle. God spends just two chapters (Genesis 1&2) describing the creation of the world and universe, but endless chapters describing the Temple! Why? The book of Hebrews tells us:

They [the priests] serve at a sanctuary that is a copy and shadow of what is in heaven … The law [the Temple and its worship system] is only a shadow of the good things that are coming – not the realities themselves. (Hebrews 8:5;10:1)

The Temple was a picture of Heaven, a type, a symbol. It was what shadow is to reality. It pointed in earthly terms and images to something heavenly and beyond our ability to conceive.

I am urging a holy boldness here! Take what God has given to you in the Bible and use it to consider Heaven. Don't hold back. If God gives us a glorious earthly Temple as a picture of Heaven, then marvel at it. If streets of gold, then ponder them. Compare them to the muddy ruts of this earth. Consider a place so wonderful that God uses *gold* for tarmac! If God gives us a crystal river, compare it to the often-polluted streams of this world. If He tells us of fragrant incense, consider a place with no stench of sin and death. If we read of choirs and music and rapturous worship, then glory in them as images, shadows of something far greater to come.

I also beg for a reverent humility here. Don't dare to think yourself so advanced, so wise, that you scoff at such imagery as beneath you or too primitive for your tastes. You know nothing about unseen things, and neither do I, except what God has condescended in His wisdom to show us. To consider ourselves to be somehow too high for God's wisdom is to imitate Satan's folly.

Dare to consider our risen and glorified Jesus. Remind yourself that one day you will see Him and be like Him. He will soon "transform our lowly bodies so that they will be like His glorious body" (Philippians 3:21). Do not push the God who has come so near in Jesus far away by refusing to believe that "when Christ appears, we shall be like him, for we shall see him as he is" (1 John 3:2). Think of the day when your body will be glorified. No more pain and weakness! Imagine a glorified mind, able to "know fully" (1 Corinthians 13:12). Consider the saints in Glory. Perfect in love, "from every tribe and language and people and nation" (Revelation 5:9). Look with your eyes of faith to the heavenly Church, already triumphant. Consider "Mount Zion, the city of the living God, the heavenly Jerusalem [and] thousands upon thousands of angels in joyful assembly [and] the church of the firstborn, whose names are written in heaven [and] God, the Judge of all [and] the spirits of the righteous made perfect [and] Jesus the mediator of a new covenant, and ... the sprinkled blood that speaks a better word than the blood of Abel" (Hebrews 12:22-24).

I could go on and on! The Bible has so many images of Heaven to inform our minds and warm our hearts. Read it with a deliberate intent to see and learn all that you can of your heavenly home. Your Heavenly Father loves you and wants you now, today, to anticipate with joy what His Son is preparing for you (John 14:3)!

2) Learn to *think from the earthly to the heavenly.* If you can learn to think from the ordinary to the extraordinary, or from

the lesser to the greater, you will find help for heavenly thinking all around you.

God has given us a seemingly endless bounty of delights here on earth. What an abundant God we have! These delights can either become snares to our souls – idols - if we end our joy with them, or inspire us to higher thinking. If you find delight in your food, you can either eat it like a mindless pagan, with no thought of anything but the food itself (as an animal does), or use it to raise your thankful heart heavenward and consider the delights that await you when you feast with Jesus at His table in Heaven. Let your earthly bread remind you of The Bread of Life. Thirsty? Let your drink speak to you of a day when no one will ever thirst again. Even if just for a moment your thoughts have been raised heavenward, God is blessed and are you edified.

Let a beautiful sunset, mountain, or river remind you to think of the wonders that await you in a glorified new creation. That wonderful house? How can it compare to the house which Jesus prepares for us in Heaven? That fair city? Imagine the City of God, ever abundant with life *and* with no cemeteries, hospitals, ghettos, police!

Science and discovery? Think of the delights we now know in learning something new, of exploring and expanding your horizon of knowledge. When we push back our limits of understanding, discovering places and wonders yet unknown, the world rejoices and stands in awe. Can you imagine what it will be like when, with glorified minds, we embark on a never-ending journey of discovery with Jesus, "in whom are hidden all the treasures of wisdom and knowledge" (Colossians 2:3)? Science! Art! Music! Astronomy! We have just barely begun. What wonders await us in Jesus' Heaven! If we have such wonder in the face of human learning, what wonders will there be in the face of God?

What about the knowledge of God? Every Truth discovered in the Bible will be magnified and expanded .... dare I say ... infinitely. The discoveries of God in nature will be magnified beyond imagining, for if *these* heavens declare His glory (Psalm 19:1), what of the heavens which are to come? Here we are seeing darkly, then in full brightness. What we have learned of God, Father, Son, and Spirit now is true and sufficient for today, but hardly exhaustive, for with our God we will find endless treasures and He will fill us "with joy in [His] presence, with eternal pleasures at [His] right hand" (Psalm 16:11).

Think of relationships. If human love and friendship can bring such joy here, even though alloyed with sin, misunderstanding, and self, what joys will they bring in Heaven, where no sin and self can mar them? More, if human friendship can be so wonderful, what will full friendship with God be like? How our souls will be at last satisfied! Whatever love we have begun to experience here is but a faint foretaste of what awaits us:

"Father, I want those you have given me to be with me where I am, and to see my glory, the glory you have given me because you loved me before the creation of the world. Righteous Father... I have made you known to them ... in order that the love you have for me may be in them and that I myself may be in them." (John 17:24-26)

In learning to think from the lesser to the greater, use everything to lift your hearts and minds heavenward throughout your day. This applies not only to good and pleasant things, but to trials and tragedies as well. When sorrow comes your way, consider that day when sorrow will be unknown. When frustrations are yours, lift your thoughts heavenward and console your heart with the knowledge that annoyances are a part of this fallen world, but not of the world to come. Death, sickness, pain, sadness, sin, even these can be used to lift you to Heaven and encourage your heart on your journey there.

When you see the nations in a rage and the love of man growing cold, consider that day when all the redeemed nations will bring their tributes to their King, when wars have ceased forever, and where all hearts are warmed with love for each other with the ever-present love of God. Do you hear of a persecuted Church in a hateful land? Is your heart broken with the news of brothers and sisters imprisoned, tortured, and martyred? Even then you can lift your thoughts to a day when the entire Church is in triumph, their blood has been avenged, and their joys are without boundaries.

3) Learn to *use God's present mercies to you as sureties of His greater mercies to come.* How often has God been good to you? Think of His abounding providences to you and to others: the wonders of nature and this amazing world – birdsong and fragrance, gentle breezes and wondrous colours. If God pours such mercy and beauty upon sinful man, what must He have in store for His redeemed sons and daughters?

What of His daily goodness to you personally? What about the deliverances and the handfuls of grace He has left here and there for you? Remember the dear people He has brought your way and how His love for you has been manifested through them. Consider the many times He has delivered you from trials, forgiven your sin, saved you from foolishness. Think of the days of feasting, the warm evenings, the cool mornings. Don't forget the times He has been with you in pain and mourning, when His Gospel has been to you a deep well of

195

comfort. If God is so good to you now, while your heart is so cold and your affections so wayward, what will He be to you in Glory when grace has finished its work?

Consider how He has ministered Himself to you through your Bible, and by His Spirit, how much you have already learned about your wonderful God! Recall the times when that book has refreshed you, corrected you, and fed you, and how it has daily been your guide. What a mercy that He has given you teachers and friends who have helped you see Jesus in the Scriptures! Don't forget the times when your soul has taken even a little flight as the truth of God has been made known through something as mundane as ink and paper. If that be the case now, what will the very beholding of Jesus be to you?

Consider the Church - this fellowship of faltering disciples. Think of how dear they have been to you. Remember how many times they have refreshed your spirit, met your needs, and patiently loved you. Bring to mind those moments of sweet fellowship which have been a true foretaste of what is ahead. You can even use the fractures and divisions (how painful!) to help you hunger for that day when all will be healed in Jesus. If God can so bless us today with His weak, frail Body, what blessings will we know in Heaven from His perfect Church?

If my pilgrimage through this barren land has been strewn with so much mercy, what will I find in my home in Heaven?

So, friend, learn this art of using what God has given you to visit Heaven. Take heart and trust me: The smallest true thought of God and His Glory is of more value than all the treasures of any earthly kingdom. The briefest groan after Jesus and His Heaven is of greater worth to God and your soul than all the applause the world can give.

Scriptures to Ponder:

Great is the Lord, and most worthy of praise,
in the city of our God, his holy mountain.
Beautiful in its loftiness,
the joy of the whole earth,
like the heights of Zaphon is Mount Zion,
the city of the Great King.
God is in her citadels;
he has shown himself to be her fortress.
(Psalm 48:1-3)

Then I saw 'a new heaven and a new earth,' for the first heaven and the first earth had passed away, and there was no longer any sea. I saw the Holy City, the new Jerusalem, coming down out of heaven from God, prepared as a bride beautifully dressed for her husband. And I heard a loud voice from the throne saying, 'Look! God's dwelling-place is now among the people, and he will dwell with them. They will be his people, and God himself will be with them and be their God. (Revelation 21:1-3)

I know that my redeemer lives,
and that in the end he will stand on the earth.
And after my skin has been destroyed,
yet in my flesh I will see God;
I myself will see him
with my own eyes – I, and not another.
How my heart yearns within me!
(Job 19:25-27)

Questions to Consider:

1) Discuss the grace and wisdom of God in speaking to us about Heaven in words and pictures that we can understand?

2) Discuss ways you have used the ordinary to ponder the extraordinary, the earthly to ponder the heavenly? Can you see how God has ordained all things to help you think of, love, and prepare for Heaven?

3) How can the present faithfulness of God to you, through His providential care, His Word, and His Church, encourage you to anticipate Heaven?

4) How can a blessing become either a hindrance or a help in raising your affections heavenward?

Chapter Eighteen

Preaching to Yourself

Now, I am not going to rush this. You have read this far, so I take it you are not in a hurry, nor about to quit! It is my concern that you master the art of heavenly thinking. I want to present you with a tool, one already in your tool box, and you have used it before, but perhaps only with worldly projects. It is time to use it for a heavenly purpose. This tool is *Preaching to Yourself.* I want to show you how to use it to affect your *love, desire, hope, boldness,* and *joy.*

You will recall that I have drawn a direct link between the mind and the heart. Christian meditation ... what I dare to call visiting Heaven ... bears no resemblance to emptying your mind. Exactly the opposite, it is bringing all the energy of thought to task. It is using the revelation which God has given us, both the general revelation of nature and the special revelation of Scripture, to persuade the heart to rejoice in what God is preparing for us - and preparing us for. It is not irrational but completely rational. It sometimes means presenting God's case to your lazy, worldly, distracted self and disputing God's arguments against yourself until God wins. It can be a wrestling match! Other times it can be a sweet time spent embracing welcomed truths to the comfort of our souls.

In any case, meditation puts biblical reasoning and thinking in its rightful place of authority. So often biblical truth sleeps while sensuality wakes and dominates. But it is our duty to rouse our thinking every day, many times a day, that it – like Samson finally aroused - might break the chains of lust and worldliness.

We have seen that God has given us, both in nature and Scripture, a superabundance of wonderful helps to raise our thoughts, and then our hearts, heavenward. These deliver us from fantasy, lust, and mere animal responses to what is all around us. They raise our affections to a more noble place (Aren't you ready for this, being sick and tired of your low, lustful thoughts and affections?) Meditation on Heaven will slay the Goliath of folly as surely as David's stone did slay the foolish giant before him. It will move you from wickedness to holiness, for wicked men are so not because they cannot think, but because they do not think about the right things!

One final word before I move toward more specifics: Be patient here. Do not be like the child who digs up the seed every day to see if it has sprouted, or who removes the plaster every hour to see if the wound has healed. A few steps of running might break a sweat, but a long walk will warm the heart. We need to move from sudden and brief thoughts of Heaven (as good as they might be) to a life spent near to the Throne of God. And God is willing for you to be there, for:

> *Even the sparrow has found a home,*
> *and the swallow a nest for herself ...*
> *a place near your altar...*
> (Psalm 84:3)

Preaching the Gospel to yourself is not as strange as it may sound. David preached to himself. Psalm 103 is a whole sermon self-preached. It really should be our regular habit. As a father preaches to his children, and a pastor to his flock, so we should learn to preach to ourselves the wonders of Jesus, His Gospel, and Heaven. In preaching to yourself, you are applying Truth to your mind, knowing that it will work its way to your heart.

One good dose of Truth might afford you hours, days, even years of sermons preached to yourself! Like a barrister presenting a case before a jury, plead the arguments of God against your cold, worldly heart. Comfort your hurting heart with the consolations of the Gospel. Warm yourself. Warn yourself. Discover all that you can about God, His Gospel, and His Heaven in the Bible. Learn the ways of Jesus. See His love for sinners and His hatred of dead, formal religion. Consider every image of Heaven and your Rest. Ask yourself: "Is there anything in this world as wonderful as this picture of Heaven?" "Is there anything on earth worthy of forfeiting Heaven?" "If I have Jesus and His Heaven will I lack anything?" Find all the images of Jesus and His ways in the Bible and meditate upon them until they have influence upon your heart. Recall God's past dealings with you. Think of how God has worked in history and in the lives of others. Lay the entire case out and weigh it all in light of eternity.

Learn to do this often. There are endless Scriptures which will give you weapons to use against your worldliness and balms to apply to your wounds. Learn to listen to sermons as if your very life depends upon hearing well. Learn to get alone with God and His Word and Spirit expecting Him to speak. Learn to take Truth heard and read and apply it diligently. Be on the lookout for droppings from Heaven in the Bible and learn to survey those truths from every angle, preaching to yourself as a passionate pastor to a needy congregation:

> *Within your temple, O God,*
> *we meditate on your unfailing love.*
> *... Walk about Zion, go around her,*
> *count her towers, consider well her ramparts...*
> (Psalm 48:9;12,13a)

201

Take walks and preach to yourself. When you are lying on your bed, or going about your business, recall what you read in the Bible about Heaven and tell yourself about it again. Learn to use your memory like a treasure chest of Truth. When troubles are attacking or pleasure is threatening, preach to yourself! Let faith lead you into the presence of God and hear it say to you: "Here is the One who made the universe with nothing but His Word." "Here is the very Fountain of Life." "Behold the God who has saved you by His grace and who has loved you from eternity to eternity." Learn to recall what you have discovered in your private meditation in every sphere of daily life. Bring out some gem and gaze upon it for a few minutes until your heart is warmed, your pace is strengthened, and your path is straightened.

In preaching to yourself, you can expect:

1) Your *Love* to be kindled. You have loved the things of this world long enough. Hours spent dwelling on the trifling and transitory have burned over much of your heart.

Is it not time to see your heart ignited by the flame of God's love? Remember that our hearts respond to our minds. Even when vile people think about vile things their hearts are warmed. In your life, if you think about something that you love, your heart responds. Our spiritual lives are no different.

Present Truth to yourself until your heart begins to stir! Oh, our hearts! They can be so difficult. But we can take them in hand and bring a response from them. Preaching is like the crushing of spices – the marvelous fragrances of Truth are released for our hearts to enjoy. Learn the discipline of taking your thoughts higher ... away from this fallen world until you can say with the Psalmist:

My heart is stirred by a noble theme
as I recite my verses for the king;
(Psalm 45:1)

2) Your *Desire* to be heightened. You have had enough low worldly desire. Constantly meditating upon worthless things has gotten you used to the valleys and afraid of the mountains. It is time now to set your godly desires above, where Christ is.

Watch your desire follow your love! If love be ignited, desire will rise on the warm currents to new heights. Think of the incomparable beauty of the Lord! Consider the vast angelic host and the Church in Glory who right now are enjoying God in fullness. Tell yourself of the difference in their state and yours until you desire theirs more than yours and can say with Paul: "I desire to depart and be with Christ, which is better by far" (Philippians 1:23). Here you are often sinning. There they are ever praising. Here you are often sighing. There they are ever rejoicing. You have much pain with moments of pleasure. They have endless pleasure with no pain. Here you are entangled with the world. There they are enthralled with the love of God. You see God dimly. They see His beautiful face. You still know cares and fears. They know only peace and joy. You still wipe away your tears. God has wiped theirs away forever. Your heart's love is extinguished in a moment. Their hearts are aflame evermore.

Preach the wonders of Christ and His Heaven to yourself until your heart ignites with love and your desires soar to new realms. Then you will say with David:

I have seen you in the sanctuary
and beheld your power and your glory.

203

*Because your love is better than life,
my lips will glorify you.* (Psalm 63:2,3)

3) Your *Hope* will be enlivened. Enough time has been spent hoping in vain things that cannot deliver life! Perhaps like so many around you, lifeless things have all but killed hope within you.

Preaching the wonders of God to yourself will bring hope to life. Where hope is dead, there is no joy in your duties and no adventure in your spirit. Where is the farmer who sows without hope, or the soldier who wages war where all is hopeless? Hope gives courage and boldness in the face of impossibilities.

Let faith bring you into the presence of the God of Hope. Once there, look at His promises for you and His heart toward you. What else do you need to bring hope to life? Show your soul the mercies of God in the Bible. See there that His good plans for you are not only possible, even probable, but certain. Remind yourself of the Lord's faithfulness to this very day. Tell yourself how He has guided you and surrounded you with His love. Ask yourself: "Has Jesus ever failed me, even in my darkest moments?" Such hope – confident assurance in the character and promises of God – will give you a boldness to live for Jesus otherwise unknown.

Before you are trials and tears, challenges and adventures. Ahead are a funeral and a grave. But beyond is a certain Rest and a Crown of Righteousness. Preach to yourself until you can say:

*No one who hopes in you will ever be put to shame... Guide me in
your truth and teach me, for you are God my Saviour, and
my hope is in you all day long.* (Psalm 25: 3;5)

4) Then *Boldness* will be yours. How long will you live in fear? How long will you hold back when Christ is calling you forward?

How can one be bold where love and desire and hope are absent? How can one be anything but bold when they are present? David, when at rock-bottom, strengthened himself in his God and took bold action (1 Samuel 30:6ff). How we need saints of courage and resolve today! Preaching the wonders of Jesus and His Heaven to yourself cannot help but put cowardice to flight and embolden you. Challenge your fear from your own private pulpit: "How can I lose when Jesus is my Champion?" "Why do I live in fear when I have a conquering God who is for me?" "Am I not invited to live and war in the strength that God promises to supply?" "Why do I cower in my own weakness when I can run in Christ's strength?"

Press the hope-filled promises of God to your soul: "The Good Shepherd is *my* Shepherd and he will never fail me. Surely then I too can say: 'I can do all this through him who gives me strength'" (Philippians 4:13). "The enemy has to defeat the Shepherd before he can touch the sheep, and the Lord Jesus has already overwhelmed him on the cross." "If I am sure of Heaven, purchased and secured for me, then I can say with David:

When I am afraid, I put my trust in you.
In God, whose word I praise –
in God I trust and am not afraid.
What can mere mortals do to me?"
(Psalm 56:3,4)

5) Finally, *Joy* will grow. Are you tired of joyless religion when Christ promises His joy to be in you (John 15:11)? Is it not tragic to live in joyless defeat when Jesus and His Heaven are your purchased, promised possession?

Love, Desire, Hope, Boldness, and Joy are yours when you preach the Gospel and all its wonders to yourself. Applying Truth to your mind until it cascades into your heart is transformational.

Jesus wants to fill you with His Joy:

*I have told you this so that my joy may be in you and that your joy may be complete ... Ask and you will receive, and your joy will be complete ... but I say these things ... so that they may have the full measure of my **joy** within them.* (John 15:11;16:24;17:3)

Meditating upon Heaven, learning to think scripturally about eternity, cannot help but produce Joy within you. You may be facing very great trials today. There may be no earthly end in sight. But "our light and momentary troubles are achieving for us an eternal glory that far outweighs them all" (2 Corinthians 4:17). Therefore, Joy can be yours today. Take yourself in your sanctified imagination to the Land of Promise and Plenty. See the Crystal River flowing from God's Throne and the ever-abundant Tree of Life. Walk around the New Jerusalem! Taste of the feast that awaits. See the abundant joy of the People of God from every tribe and tongue and nation. Look for pain, sin, death, and sickness, but you will not find it. Where are the hospitals? The sick-beds? The graveyards? Only Life, Joy, and Righteousness will be in Jesus' Heaven. See Jesus, so willing and ready to give you all that is His, for you truly are – by grace – an heir with Him of all things. Hear Him say to you: "'Do not be afraid, little flock, for your Father has been pleased to give you the kingdom. Sell your possessions and give to the poor. Provide purses for yourselves that will not wear out, a treasure in heaven that will never fail, where no thief comes near and no moth destroys. For where your treasure is, there your heart will be also" (Luke 12:32-34).

Go there today in your spirit and get your Joy! Stay there until you can say with the Psalmist:

Thou hast put gladness in my heart, more than in the time that
their corn and their wine increased.
(Psalm 4:7 KJV)

Scriptures to Ponder:

But David found strength in the Lord his God.
(1 Samuel 30:6)

I rise before dawn and cry for help;
I have put my hope in your word.
My eyes stay open through the watches of the night,
that I may meditate on your promises.
(Psalm 119:147,148)

May the God of hope fill you with all joy and peace as you trust in
him, so that you may overflow with hope by the power of the
Holy Spirit.
(Romans 15:13)

Why, my soul, are you downcast? Why so disturbed within me?
Put your hope in God, for I will yet praise him, my Saviour and
my God. (Psalm 42:5)

Questions to Consider:

1) Have you ever preached to yourself before?

2) How important is it to know the Bible if you are going to strengthen yourself in the Lord?

3) If you have a willing God and a Bible, what keeps you from meditating upon God's purchased and promised Heaven until you are transformed in Love, Desire, Hope, Boldness, and Joy?

Chapter Nineteen

Be Encouraged!

As we come to our close together, may I take a last opportunity to encourage you in this great adventure? Let me remind you that this is not just some self-indulgent exercise. Preparing yourself for Heaven, becoming acquainted with what God has planned for you honours God, strengthens you, and makes you better able to love God and others in this life.

Without question, the happiest and most useful Christians are those who live in constant expectation and anticipation of Heaven.

Let me offer these final encouragements:

1) *You have a willing God.* God is for you. He is not stubborn or grudging in His goodness. He - Father, Son, and Holy Spirit - is an eternal community of love and joy, and He wants you to enter into His fullness. You do not have to beg Him, plead with Him, pay Him, or cajole Him. He has made the way, a "new and living way," (Hebrews 10:20) through Himself in Jesus Christ. He has made you heir of all things in Jesus, who is even now preparing His Heaven for you and you for His Heaven. He is superabundant in His grace and you will never exhaust His love. The fight for your heart is winable because He is for you, and:

If God is for us, who can be against us? He who did not spare his own Son, but gave him up for us all – how will he not also, along with him, graciously give us all things? (Romans 8:31,32)

2) *God has given you every resource to win the battle for your heart.* Yes, it is true, your greatest foe will more often than not be your own heart. I have already told you this, so I will not belabour the point too long. You heart will sometimes sleep, other times it will revolt. It will sometimes be like a wayward servant, other times like a lazy employee. You cannot leave it to itself, for it will love everything but God and Heaven. It will produce idols like a factory produces goods.

You will have to correct it, awaken it, chide it, and dare I say, grab it by the scruff of the neck and make it obey your will.

But you have God on your side, and you can, in the name of Jesus, take authority over your wayward heart. Make it obey you! Do not obey it! The Bible is full of sad stories of those who let their hearts go their own way: Samson, Uzziah, Solomon, Judas, Demas. Take these as incentives to do the opposite. Do not let your heart loiter. March it to Jesus every day. Preach Truth to it until it warms and becomes a lover of God and Heaven.

You have the Bible, the Holy Spirit, the Church, the Atonement, your conscience, all at your disposal. Heaven waits and watches (Hebrews 12:1). You have David and Hannah, Mary and Paul, John and Daniel, and endless others who have brought their hearts to task and seen their hearts become God-loving, Heaven-aiming servants of their wills. The battle will be daily – moment by moment – but it is yours to win.

3) *Be diligent.* Be as diligent as a banker with his funds or a gardener with his garden. How our lives will be different if we will just be diligent in things that matter! So, preach Heaven to yourself. With an open Bible and a submitted heart, apply the Truth of God to your mind day by day until you become more familiar with your approaching Rest than you are with the

things all about you. Call out to God for help. Commit a season every day to contemplating – visiting – Heaven. Use the helps I have offered you in this book. I promise you that you will be transformed from a lover of frivolous and vain things to a lover of God and Eternal things, from a coward to a fighter for Truth, from a cold clod to a burning ember. If you fail today, there is tomorrow. Do not give up!

You will be as happy and as holy as you want to be. There is no lack in God. Those who refuse God's command to place their hearts and minds above not only make themselves miserable, but deny the whole cause of Christ the value of their Heaven-mindedness. Those who by diligence learn to live *now* in anticipation of *then* will tell you that they would not exchange their lives with those of princes or kings.

So, learn to walk everyday in the New Jerusalem. I know your heart is not what you want it to be. But Jesus loves you and awaits your company. Do not rest until you find yourself in the suburbs of Heaven and those about you see that Christianity is, for you, not just duties and ideas, but a heavenly life.

****

"Heavenly Father! God of our hearts! You are the deepest need of my life. God! Call this drowsy, mixed heart upward to Yourself. Do Your supernatural work in me! I trust in Your good plans for me, and in Your heart towards me.

I worship and bless You for being a willing God. Do not let me be a lover of this world more than a lover of You and Your world to come. Keep me jealously for Yourself! Whatever it takes to make me long for You, and stay close to You, do it, Lord. Save me from time-wasting and foolish living. Remind me often, Lord, of how near Heaven is, and at what cost I have been redeemed from a deserved Hell.

On that day when you come for me, Lord, let me be found looking, waiting, doing, yearning. Let me not be a wicked and lazy servant, but a diligent and longing son. Lord, may those who read these words which I have written see them not merely as my mind's achievement, but as my heart's longing for them. Lord Jesus! May these words not be a witness against me as words of pride and accomplishment, but of a longing heart. May they therefore be a channel of Your grace. As such, may they touch the dear reader, and be a savour of life both to them and to me.

Amen, and Glory to God in the Highest!"

Now to him who is able to do immeasurably more than all we ask or imagine, according to his power that is at work within us, to him be glory in the church and in Christ Jesus throughout all generations, for ever and ever! Amen.
(Ephesians 3:20,21)

Appendix

Richard Baxter's Introductory Letter to His Parish[□]

To Dearly Beloved Friends,
The Inhabitants of the Borough and Foreign of Kidderminster
Both Magistrates and People

My Dear Friends,

If either I or my labours have anything of public use or worth it is wholly, though not only, yours; and I am convinced, by Providence, that it is the will of God that it should be so. This I clearly discerned in my first coming to you, in my former abode with you, and in the time of my forced absence from you. ... Your free invitation of my return, your obedience to my doctrine, the strong affection which I have yet towards you above all people, and the general, hearty return of love which I find from you, do all to persuade me that I was sent into the world especially for the service of your souls. And that even when I am dead I might yet be a help to your salvation, the Lord hath forced me, quite beside my own resolution, to write this treatise, and leave it in your hands. It was far from my thoughts ever to have become thus public, and burdened the world with any writings of mine; ... but see how God overrulleth and crosseth our resolutions.

Being in my quarters, far from home, cast into extreme languishing by the sudden loss of about a gallon of blood, and after many years' foregoing weaknesses, and having no acquaintance about me, nor any books but my Bible, and living in constant expectation of death, I bent my thoughts on my Everlasting Rest; and because my memory, through extreme weakness, was imperfect, I took my pen and began to draw up my own funeral sermon, or some helps for my own meditation of heaven, to sweeten both the rest of my life and my death. In this condition God was pleased to continue me for about five months, from home, where, being able for nothing else, I went on with this work, which so lengthened to this where you see. It is no wonder, therefore, if I be too abrupt in the

---

beginning, seeing I then intended but the length of a sermon or two. Much less may you wonder if the whole be very imperfect, seeing that it was written, as it were with one foot in the grave, by a man betwixt the living and the dead, that wanted strength of nature to quicken invention or affection, and had no book but his Bible while the chief part of it was finished, nor had any mind of human ornaments if he had been furnished. But O how sweet this Providence now to my review, which so happily forced me to that work of meditation which I had formerly found so profitable to my soul, and showed me more mercy in depriving me of other helps than I was aware of, and hath caused my thoughts to feed on this heavenly subject, which hath more benefited me than all the studies of my life!

And now, dear friends, such as it is I here offer it to you; and upon the bended knees of my soul I offer up my thanks to the merciful God who hath fetched up both me and it, as from the grave, for your service; who reversed the sentence of present death, which, by the ablest physicians, was passed upon me; who interrupted my public labours for a time, that he might force me to do you a more lasting service, which, else, I had never been like to have attempted. ...

Your most affectionate, though unworthy teacher,

Rich. Baxter

Kidderminster
15th January 1649

Afterword

We need books like this because of the Bible. This book made all sorts of future-oriented texts come to life for me:

John 6.40. One day I'll die. Then one day Christ Himself will personally raise me. The King of all kings will call me by name and raise me.

John 14.3. Right now He is preparing a place for me, such that I will be where He is. Again, given the not insignificant differences between us - this is stunning.

John 16.22. What a game-changer! In Christ, my present sorrow will soon end. I'm heading for indestructible, so-happy-I'm-crying, make-your-cheeks-ache-beaming heart rejoicing.

Hebrews 9.29. The distinguishing feature of those to be saved is being a man or woman "eagerly waiting for him". Really, it is.

We need books like this because John makes me yearn for heaven and equips me with a whole wealth of tools (Chapters 14-17) to do so more.

We need books like this because we are not doing very well at esteeming one another. Enslaved to measuring immediate responses, it is all but impossible to sincerely love our brothers and sisters in Christ for more than a week or two. Their flaws are just so annoying. Many of us are so immature and so damaged, that we may never be able to recognize the banquet of love others attempt to spread out for us. How to persevere? This book stubbornly refuses to deny the reality of future rest and reward - and implicitly presses us into loving the ugly, weak, and insignificant for the long haul (Matthew 25.40).

We need books like this because reaching the unreached and unengaged is probably going to feel unrewarding sooner or later. Amy Carmichael, missionary to India was told "We neither want nor need your Jesus" almost century ago, and the same pushback is felt the world over.

Even where local churches do exist, problems ranging from irritating peevishness, to full-blown wolves in sheep's clothing abound. The best and most sincere efforts get shipwrecked. Week after week. Year after year. All five senses urge for despair. Paragraphs like the following revive fainting souls:

"He told us plainly that it was better for us if He, for a season, left us. "But very truly I tell you, it is for your good that I am going away. Unless I go away, the Advocate [Holy Spirit] will not come to you; but if I go, I will send him to you." (John 16:7). We have to trust Him for this. *He* knows that it was best to leave us for a season, and send His Holy Spirit to us. *He* knows that He has accomplished His work of redemption. *He* knows that it is better for us that He intercede for us than to be bodily present with us. *He* knows that He had to go and prepare a place for us. *He* knows our time here is short and that we will soon be with Him. *He* knows that there are precious others ... countless redeemed souls ... now in Heaven rejoicing with Him. *He* knows that it is better for us to walk now by faith than by sight. **And *we* need to rest in what *He* knows**. (from Chapter 5 - emphasis mine).

It's no secret that Baxter's very real brush with death and pain gave birth to the project. "I preached as never sure to preach again, and as a dying man to dying men" may well have become a cliche, but for Baxter it was surely wasn't.

Nor for John Gillespie.

Three weeks before John and I were due to do a conference together, he called me with some news. His heart was not able to do what it should, and he was now required to wear a 'life-vest" complete with built-in defibrillator 24/7. His cardiologist had told him to prepare for the worst. After a couple of operations to fit enough technology to qualify him as a cyborg, I'm happy to report he tells me he feels fine.

If, then you detect a certain life and death intensity in these pages, you now know why.

Finally, a note about reading this book. I haven't asked John, but I don't expect he'd mind if you didn't read it all at one sitting. If you dip into it - that's ok. You'll come up with gold more often than not.

"Oh, for a day when pride, laziness, coldness of heart, mixed motives, alloyed love, desire for place and power... Oh for a day when these are *gone*! That day is soon to come! We will never again grieve the Spirit of God! There will never again be a word of gossip or even the slightest intent of it. No intrigue, no posturing, no hint of hypocrisy. **Imagine relationships**

without a shadow of manipulation or selfishness. What a day!"
(Chapter 5, "Four Foundations of Our Rest")

Amen.

David Bhadreshwar
Missionary and Church Planter
Lima, January 2019.